Afghan
Food &
Cookery

T0268874

Afghan Food & Cookery

Noshe Djan

BY
HELEN SABERI

WITH THE HELP OF
NAJIBA ZAKA AND SHAIMA BRESHNA

AND DRAWINGS BY
ABDULLAH BRESHNA

HIPPOCRENE BOOKS, INC.
New York

Copyright © 2000 Helen Saberi (Hippocrene Books, Inc. U.S. edition)
Fourth printing, 2007.

Drawings© 1986 Abdullah Breshna
Cover photograph© Madeline Polss

The first edition of this book was published in the U.K. under the title
Noshe Djan: Afghan Food and Cookery by Prospect Books in 1986.

All rights reserved.

For information, address:
Hippocrene Books, Inc.
171 Madison Avenue
New York, NY 10016

Library of Congress Cataloging-in-Publication Data

Saberi, Helen.
    Afghan food & cookery : = Noshe djan / by Helen Saberi, with the help of
Najiba Zaka and Shaima Breshna; and drawings by Abdullah Breshna.
        p. cm.
    ISBN-13: 978-0-7818-0807-1
    ISBN-10: 0-7818-0807-3
        1. Cookery, Afghan. I. Title: Afghan food and cookery. II. Title: Noshe
djan. III. Zaka, Najiba. IV. Breshna, Shaima. V. Title.

    TX724.5.A3 S23 2000
    641.5952--dc81   00-058200

Printed in the United States of America.

To
Alexander and Oliver

And
All the children of Afghanistan

Map of Afghanistan

CONTENTS

x Afghan Food & Cookery

ACKNOWLEDGMENTS

This book would not have been possible without the help and interest of many friends and relatives.

First of all I would like to thank my husband, Nasir, for all the help, advice, patience and especially encouragement he has given me in preparing this book. I must say he particularly enjoyed tasting all the recipes!

Special thanks are due to my sister-in-law, Najiba Zaka, and also my close friend, Shaima Breshna. Both sent me many recipes, but also advised and helped me with Afghan cooking techniques and traditions, and showed me how to make some of the more complicated dishes.

Special thanks too to Shaima's husband, Dip. Ing. Arch. Abdullah Breshna, for volunteering to provide all the lovely and unusual illustrations for the book.

Many other friends have given recipes, advice and encouragement. I should particularly like to thank Khalil and Sara Rashidzada, who invited us to their home to show me how to prepare the delicious specialty of the Uzbeks, *mantu,* and an Uzbek *pilau.* I am also grateful to Abdullah and Parwin Ali, Qassim and Valerie Hachimzai, Naheed and David Knight and Mr. Abdul Ghaffour Redja.

I thank Anthony Hyman for his guidance and advice, particularly on the introduction; and Stephen Keynes for his help in getting the book published.

For so often looking after my children, especially baby Oliver, so that I could get on with the final testing of recipes and typing of the manuscript, I should like to express my gratitude to my mother, Hilda Canning, and my friends Carole Cooles and Louise Boyd. Young Alexander must also be thanked for his patience and understanding when I was too busy to help with homework or take him swimming.

Finally I would like to thank everyone at Prospect Books, especially Alan and Jane Davidson, not only for undertaking to publish this book and giving their expert advice, but also for their sympathy to the Afghan cause. I am particularly indebted to my copy-editor, Idonea Muggeridge, for her help and enthusiasm, all the more appreciated as I had never written a book before.

ACKNOWLEDGMENTS TO SECOND EDITION

Over the years, since the first edition of this book was published, I have been able, with the help of many friends and relatives, to increase my knowledge of Afghan food, traditions, and customs. Many Afghans have generously given me their recipes and they are included in this book. For these new recipes and information I am particularly indebted to my sister-in-law Najiba Zaka, Shaima Breshna, Gul Jan Kabiri, Kaka Noor Saberi, Aziza Ashraf, Mahwash Amani, Zobeida Sekanderi, Lila, Rahila Reshnou, Homa Rundell, Nafisa Yahyaee, Maleka Ibrahimi and Fatima Gailani.

My thanks continue to go to all the people who helped me with the first edition, and particularly to Abdullah Breshna who once again generously volunteered to do the illustrations. I especially like the new drawings of the donkey seller and the scene of making rosewater in the garden. They bring back such evocative memories of my nine years in Afghanistan. All the illustrations capture the flavor and character of Afghanistan so beautifully.

I would like to take this opportunity to thank those people who gave such generous and supportive reviews of the first edition: Claudia Roden, Barbara Santich, Shona Crawford Poole, Paul Levy, Miriam Poulunin, Jill Tilsley-Benham, John Birch, Faye Maschler, Ray Sokolov, Derek Cooper, Julie Sahni, Kerry Connor, Dolf Riks and Rosemary Clancy.

Gratitude and love also go to my sister-in-law Michèle Hachim-Saberi, who volunteered to translate *Noshe Djan* into French and thanks to Wali Nouri for arranging its publication in France to help the organization, AFRANE. I thank Antonia Fumagalli, who not only volunteered to translate my book into Italian to help the Afghan cause, but also found a publisher, Piemme. Harriet Sandys, Afghan Aid, and the Swedish Committee were particularly active in selling my book to raise funds for humanitarian aid and charity work inside Afghanistan.

I am grateful to all my friends and relatives who have taken such a lively and sympathetic interest in Afghan affairs and cuisine over the years. I would particularly like to thank Tony and

Hilary Hyman, Don and Sylvia Barton, Jim and Paula Cullen, David and Naheed Knight, Qassim and Valerie Hachimzai, Abdul Ghaffour Redja, Ben and Sarah Tomsett, Norman and Jacky Pritchard, Robin and Carol Debell, Bob and Carole Cooles, Laura Mason, Anissa Helou, Russell Harris, Ove Fosså and Charles Perry.

My heartfelt thanks and gratitude once again go Alan and Jane Davidson who have not only continued to be sympathetic and interested in Afghan affairs but have encouraged and advised me continuously over the last thirteen years. For the last seven I have worked alongside Alan on his magnum opus, *The Oxford Companion to Food*. It was a great honor and pleasure to do this. I have learned so much and enjoyed the opportunity to ensure that Afghanistan and Afghan dishes are mentioned in the book approximately ten times more often than would otherwise have been the case!

Heartfelt thanks are also due to Tom Jaine for spurring me on to produce this second edition and for his part in bringing about the separate edition by Hippocrene Books in the United States. I thank all those involved at Hippocrene, particularly Carol Chitnis, the Managing Editor and my copyeditor, Karen Fraley.

Finally, my love and gratitude go to my husband Nasir, who has not only painstakingly helped me work out recipes from memories he has of his childhood, when he used to watch his grandmother or mother cook, but has continued with characteristic patience and enthusiasm to help, advise and encourage me. I am deeply indebted to him.

Donkey seller.

FURTHER READING

As the acknowledgments on the previous page show, I have learned from people rather than books, and there are few books, in any language, which contain information about Afghan cookery. This short list includes some that I have consulted, and a few that would be useful to anyone wishing to know more about Afghanistan.

Afghanzada, Abdullah. *Local Dishes of Afghanistan* (in Farsi). Kabul, 1974.

Aitchison, Dr. J.E.T. *Notes on the Products of Western Afghanistan and North-Eastern Persia*. Edinburgh, 1890.

American Women's Association. *Kabul Gorgers*. Kabul, 1978.

Davidson, Alan. *The Oxford Companion to Food*. Oxford University Press: Oxford, 1999.

Dorje, Rinjing. *Food in Tibetan Life*. Prospect Books: London, 1985.

Dupree, Louis. *Afghanistan*. Princeton University Press: New Jersey, 1973. An encyclopedic work.

Dupree, Nancy. *An Historical Guide to Afghanistan*. 2nd ed. Afghan Tourist Organisation: Kabul, 1977.

Elphinstone, Mountstuart. *An Account of the Kingdom of Caubul* (reprint of 1839). Oxford University Press: Karachi, 1972.

Husain, S. A. *Muslim Cooking of Pakistan*. Sh. Muhammad Ashraf: Lahore, 1974.

Jaffrey, Madhur. *Indian Cookery*. BBC: London, 1982.

Malos, Tess. *Middle East Cookbook*. Summit Books: Sydney, 1979. Has 20 pages on Afghanistan.

McKellar, Doris, compiler. *Afghan Cookery*. Afghan Book Publisher: Kabul, 1972.

Michaud, Roland and Sabrina. *Caravans to Tartary*. Thames and Hudson: London, 1978. Many fine color photographs.

———. *Afghanistan*. Thames and Hudson: London, 1980. Many fine color photographs.

Ramazani, Nesta. *Persian Cookery*. University Press of Virginia, 1974.

Reejhsinghani, Aroona. *The Great Art of Mughlai Cooking.* Bell Books: New Delhi, 1979.

Roden, Claudia. *A New Book of Middle Eastern Food.* Viking: London and New York, 1985.

Sahni, Julie. *Classic Indian Cookery.* Grub Street: London, 1997.

———. *Classic Indian Vegetarian Cookery.* Grub Street: London, 1999.

Shaida, Margaret. *The Legendary Cuisine of Persia.* Lieuse Publications: Henley-on-Thames, 1992.

Watt, George. *A Dictionary of the Economic Products of India,* vols 1-6. 1889, reprinted Cosmo Publications: New Delhi, 1972.

Weidenweber, Sigrid, compiler. *The Best of Afghan Cookery—An Afghan Recipe Book.* American Aid for Afghans: Oregon, 1980.

FOREWORD

One of the main reasons for writing the first edition of this book was to record Afghan culinary traditions and recipes, which I felt might be lost due to the war in Afghanistan. I also wanted to contribute in a small way, to the Afghan cause and to help prevent Afghanistan from being forgotten. Many men, women and children were without food, medicines or shelter and the war had resulted in a massive exodus of refugees to countries all over the world and a consequent dispersal and erosion of their culture.

It was important to record the foods and traditions and recipes. Afghans certainly thought so. I was greatly heartened by the response the book has had from many of them living in different corners of the world. They sent me constructive advice and information about the variety of Afghan food and cookery which the presence of so many ethnic groups in one country has brought about. I was particularly delighted when many told me that hey had bought my book to give to their children, many of whom left Afghanistan at a very early age and did not remember much about the traditions and customs. It has been an honor and a pleasure for me to help them to know more about their own food culture and how to cook Afghan-style.

My husband has delved into his memory and produced many new delights for me, such as the jams, qormas and pilaus which his mother and grandmother used to make. He has also translated some of Abdullah Afghanzada's wonderful book, *Local Dishes of Afghanistan*, which is an almost definitive collection of Afghan foods and recipes in the Farsi language. My husband and I have adapted some of his excellent recipes to suit present day requirements, while still retaining their authenticity.

There are quite a few new recipes in this book, 70 altogether. I have replaced some recipes with better ones and I have taken account of the ingenuity of Afghan refugees in the West, such as using wonton wrappers in place of the special pastry for mantou and ashak.

This is not a scholarly work, but I have tried where possible to include interesting information about Afghan life, foods and traditions, which I have read or learned about over the years.

Since the first printing of this book, great changes have taken place in Afghanistan as a result of the devastating attack on September 11, 2001. A new and more hopeful era has begun. The Taliban have been driven away along with their allies, Al-Qaeda, and there is wide support for the interim government facing the enormous task of cementing peace and rebuilding the country.

I have had the opportunity of visiting Afghanistan twice in the last two years. They were emotional visits, tinged with sadness when I saw the amount of devastation and poverty. However, despite all the difficulties and troubles, I am optimistic for the future. People are busy rebuilding their homes, shops, and offices. The bazaars are bustling once again, street vendors sing out their wares, teahouses and restaurants are open. There are many signs of the Afghan people getting back to a normal life and their traditional ways.

It is cheering to think that readers of this book will join me in hoping that peace and stability will continue in Afghanistan, that wounds will be healed, and that the people of Afghanistan will work together with understanding and tolerance in rebuilding their beautiful country.

London, March 2004

INTRODUCTION

Afghanistan is situated at the meeting place of four major cultural areas: the Middle East, Central Asia, the Indian subcontinent and the Far East. It is because of this geographical position that Afghanistan became the crossroads for many invading armies from different places, each with their own culture. These marauding armies, often passing through Afghanistan, journeying further afield, realized the advantages of maintaining strongholds here and paused for a while.

In the fourth century B.C., Alexander the Great conquered Afghanistan on his way to India; in the thirteenth and fourteenth centuries A.D., Afghanistan was plundered by Genghis Khan and the Mongols en route to the Middle and Near East. Babur, founder of the Moghul Empire in India and a direct descendant of Genghis Khan, began his rise to power in Kabul and is buried in his favorite garden on a hill in Kabul, the Bagh-e-Babur Shah. Nader Shah Afshar invaded and conquered Afghanistan in the eighteenth century on his way to India, recruiting Afghan fighters to serve with his troops. The British in India were twice invaders in the nineteenth century.

Afghan dynasties, in their turn, have flourished and at various times extended their influence to parts of Central Asia, India, Iran and even China. From the Kushans, to the Ghaznavid sultans, to the Durrani rulers such spheres of influence have contributed much to the rich patterns of civilization.

Because of its special position in Central Asia, Afghanistan was also a crossroads on the ancient Silk Routes connecting

1

Europe with the Far East. Traders and merchants from many countries traveled there, including the famous Venetian traveler Marco Polo. This traffic brought many imported items such as Chinese tea and Indian spices, which have had a great influence on Afghan cuisine.

The numerous different ethnic groups living in Afghanistan—the Tajiks, Turkomans, Uzbeks, Baluchis, Pashtuns and Hazaras are just some of them—have also left their mark on Afghan traditions and food.

In short, Afghanistan has been a melting pot for a large number of cultures and traditions over the centuries, and these different influences can be detected in the variety of Afghan food and the regional specialities. Readers of this book will find many similarities with Greek, Turkish, Middle Eastern, Persian, Central Asian, Indian and even Far Eastern foods and dishes.

CLIMATE

Afghanistan is a land of contrasts: vast areas of scorching parched deserts, high, cold and inaccessible mountains and extensive green plains and valleys, some of which are subtropical. Generally the summers are dry and very hot and the winters very cold with heavy snowfalls especially in the mountains. It is this snow that provides the much needed water for irrigation in the late spring and summer. The plains and valleys are very fertile so long as there is water, and a wide variety of crops can be cultivated; it is these crops which determine the everyday diet of Afghans.

Cereals such as wheat, corn, barley and rice are the chief crops. Rice is grown on the terraces of the Hindu Kush in the north and in the Jalalabad area. Cotton is grown in the north and southwest of the country, and cotton factories in Kunduz and Lashkargah produce edible cottonseed oil. Sugar beet is grown mainly in the Pule Khumri/Kunduz area and is processed in the factory at Pule Khumri. Sugar cane is cultivated in the Jalalabad/ Nangarhar area.

Because the range of climatic conditions in Afghanistan is so wide, a great variety of vegetables and fruits grow in abundance. Afghanistan is particularly famous for its grapes, from which green and red raisins are produced, and for its melons.

SOCIAL CUSTOMS AND TRADITIONS

Afghanistan is a poor country but it is rich in traditions and social customs. Unfortunately it is not possible to describe the Afghan way of life in great detail in this book, but I have endeavored to pick out the most interesting and important aspects relating to food and cookery.

Hospitality is very important in the Afghan code of honor. The best possible food is prepared for guests even if other members of the family have to go without. A guest is always given a seat or the place of honor at the head of the room. Tea is served first to quench the guest's thirst. While he is drinking and chatting with his host, all the women and girls of the household are involved in the preparation of food.

The traditional mode of eating in Afghanistan is on the floor. Everyone sits around on large colorful cushions, called *toshak*. These cushions are normally placed on the beautiful carpets, for which Afghanistan is famous. A large cloth or thin mat called a *disterkhan* is spread over the floor or carpet before the dishes of food are brought. In summer, food is often served outside in the cooler night air, or under a shady tree during the day. In the depth of winter, food is eaten around the *sandali*, the traditional form of Afghan heating. A *sandali* consists of a low table covered with a large duvet called a *liaf* which is also big enough to cover the legs of the occupants, sitting on their cushions or mattresses and supported by large pillows called *balesht* or *poshty*. Under the table is a charcoal brazier called a *manqal*. The charcoal has to be thoroughly burned beforehand and covered with ashes.

Food is usually shared communally; three or four people will share one large platter of rice and individual side dishes of stew *qorma*, or vegetables. Homemade chutneys and pickles, as well as fresh *nan* (bread) usually accompany the food.

The traditional way of eating is with the right hand, and with no cutlery. Spoons may be used for puddings and teaspoons for tea. Because hands are used in eating there is a handwashing ceremony before meals and for this a special bowl and jug called a *haftawa-wa-lagan* is used. A young boy or girl member of the family brings this to the guest, and pours the water over his hands for him, catching the excess water in the bowl.

SANDALI

THE MOST ECONOMICAL AFGHAN SYSTEM OF HEATING

MANKAL = CHARCOAL CONTAINER ————
SANDALÍ = TABLE ————
LÍAF = SQUARE BLANKET ┘
TAKHTA = STONE or WOOD PLATE ┘
TOSHAK = COTTON MATTRESS ————
BALESHT or POSHTY = CUSHION ————

AFTABA - LAGAN

*The handwashing
ceremony and the*
haftawa-wa-lagan.

SPECIAL OCCASIONS AND RELIGIOUS FESTIVALS

Afghanistan is a Muslim country and religion plays a very important part in the way of life. Afghans observe all religious days and festivals, which are based on the lunar calendar.

The two most important festivals are *Eid-ul-Fitr* (also called *Eid-e-Ramazan*) and *Eid-e-Qorban* (sometimes called *Eid-ul-Adha*).

Eid-ul-Fitr, which goes on for three days, marks the end of *Ramazan,* the month of fasting, and is celebrated rather like Christmas. Children receive new clothing and families visit relatives and friends. Presents are not exchanged but in recent years the practice of sending *Eid* cards has increased considerably.

Eid-e-Qorban is the major festival marking the end of the *Haj,* the pilgrimage to Mecca, and lasts for four days. Again, children receive new clothing, and friends and relatives are visited.

At each *Eid,* tea, nuts, sweets and sugared almonds called *noql* are served to visitors and guests. Often special sweets and pastries are prepared: *halwa-e-swanak, sheer payra, goash-e-feel* and others. Many Afghans sacrifice a lamb or calf at *Eid-e-Qorban,* which takes its name from the word *qorban,* meaning sacrifice. The meat is distributed among the poor, and relatives and neighbors.

Another important day of celebration is New Year, called *Nauroz.* The Afghan New Year falls on 21 March, the spring equinox, our first day of spring. This special day, which celebrates new life, has its origins long before Islam, in the time of Zoroaster and the Zoroastrians. Special dishes and foods are made for the New Year: *kulcha Naurozee,* a biscuit made with rice flour and sometimes called *kulcha birinji;* and *miwa Naurozee,* a fruit and nut compote, also called *haft miwa* or *haft seen* by some because it contains seven *(haft)* fruits and the name of each fruit includes the Persian letter *seen. Shola-e-shireen* or *shola-e-zard,* both sweet rice dishes, are also made on this day for *Nazer,* a kind of thanksgiving (see page 10). Another traditional food at this time is *sabzi chalau* with chicken. The recipes for these dishes can be found in this book.

Samanak is another ancient dish prepared especially for New Year. About fifteen to twenty days before the New Year, wheat is planted in flower pots and from this wheat a sweet pudding is made. The preparation for this dish is elaborate.

At the New Year when everything is new and fresh and the bitter winter is finally over, Afghans like to go on picnics and many people visit holy shrines, *ziarat.*

Buzkashi is also played at New Year. It is the country's national sport and it resembles polo. *Buzkashi* literally means "goat-grabbing". The headless body of a goat, or sometimes a calf, is used in place of a ball. The game originated on the plains of Kunduz and Mazar-i-Sharif during the time of the Mongol invasions of Afghanistan, when it is said that the Mongol horsemen used (decapitated) prisoners of war instead of goats.

Children go out to fly their kites. These are made with colorful tissue paper on a light wooden frame, and the thread, specially made with ground glass, is extremely sharp. The kites "fight" each other in the air, trying to cut the thread of each other.

Afghans love an excuse for a party. Births, circumcisions, engagements and weddings are celebrated in grand style, although many of the associated customs are dying out. The birth of a child, especially the first male child is a big occasion, when many guests will be expected. Numerous dishes and specialities are prepared; *aush, ashak, boulanee,* kebabs, *pilau* and many desserts. Celebrations continue for ten days. On the third day or sometimes the sixth day, called *Shab-e-shash,* the local priest, *mullah,* comes to bless the child and the naming ceremony takes place. Relatives sit round a room and choose a name, which is then called into the baby's ear. On the tenth day *(dah)* after the birth, the mother gets up for the first time (until this time her women relatives have been looking after her and the baby) and goes to the public baths *(hamam).* This day is therefore called *Hamam-e-dah. Humarch,* a flour-based soup, which is considered a "hot" or strengthening food is served, especially to the new mother. Other traditional dishes often made specially for this occasion because of their reputed strengthening and nourishing properties are *leetee, kachee, aush* and *shola-e-olba,* the sweet rice dish with fenugreek. On the fortieth day after the birth, the sweet bread called *roht* is baked for close family relatives. *Roht* is also baked and rolled on the day the child walks for the first time.

Circumcision is another occasion which is still celebrated. Relatives and friends gather together when the male child is circumcised. Traditionally, the local barber is responsible for performing this task. On such a day kebabs are made from the fresh meat of a lamb specially sacrificed for the occasion and are served with a variety of foods.

Engagements and weddings are elaborate and many of the celebrations vary between the different ethnic groups. They also vary from city to village. Any engagement or wedding is an occasion for a large party. Engagements are called *shirnee khoree,* which literally means sweet eating. Traditionally the family of the groom bring sweets, *goash-e-feel,* presents, clothes, jewelery and other gifts for the bride's family. The bride's family in return prepares and organizes the food and the party to celebrate the occasion. Large numbers of guests, depending on the social standing and financial circumstances of the bride's family are invited. Special kitchens are often set up in order to cope with the preparation of vast amounts of food; *pilau, qorma, ashak, boulanee* and many varieties of desserts; *firni, shola,* jellies, pastries and lots of fruit. The tea *qymaq chai* is usually served.

Weddings take place in two stages: *nikah,* the religious ceremony when the marriage contract is actually signed, takes place first and is followed by *arusi,* which is a combination of wedding party and further ceremony.

At the second stage of the wedding the guests are first served with food while the bride is preparing herself in a separate room. A wide assortment of rich dishes similar to those at an engagement are served. The *arusi* ceremony usually takes place quite late in the evening and after the inevitable tea.

The bride and bridegroom are then brought together for the first time (the bride was not present at the religious ceremony—her signing of the contract was done by proxy). The groom sits on a raised platform called *takht* (throne) and the bride approaches, heavily veiled with female relatives holding the Qor'an (Koran) over her head. The bride joins the groom and a mirror is placed before them. Several ceremonies then take place involving the tasting of *sharbat* (a fruit drink) and *molida,* a flour-based, powdery sweet. Henna is painted on the couple's hands or fingers. Sugared almonds *(noql)* symbolizing fruitfulness and prosperity and other sweets, symbolizing happiness, are then showered over the newlyweds, rather like the western tradition of throwing confetti.

Another less happy occasion when many friends and relatives get together is for a death. Food is prepared for the mourning family and guests, many of whom will stay for a number of days with the bereaved family. On the first Friday after a death, and on the fortieth day, relatives and friends gather together to hear the

Qor'an being read, usually by the local priest *(mullah),* after which food is served.

Another custom which perhaps should be mentioned here is the *Shab-e-mourdaha,* which literally means night of the dead. These special nights are held on the eve of an *Eid* and New Year. The dead of the family are remembered and *halwa* is made and distributed to the poor.

Nazer is another important religious custom. It is practiced by all, whether rich or poor, and is a thanksgiving that can take place on any day. *Nazer* is offered for a number of reasons like the safe return of a relative after a journey or recovery from a serious illness. Another important reason for *nazer* is to mark a visit to a holy shrine and the fulfilment of a prayer made on this pilgrimage. For these occasions special dishes such as *halwa* or *shola* are cooked and distributed to the poor. The most simple offering for *nazer* is to buy a dozen fresh *nan* and hand pieces out to passers-by in the street. The more affluent sacrifice a lamb or calf. *Nazer* is always accepted graciously as it has such religious significance.

My mother-in-law used to make a large pot of *halwa.* Portions of this were placed on a large piece of fresh *nan.* A large tray was set up and a servant or member of the family went out in the street and offered it to anyone passing by. We also sent it to our neighbors.

Nazer is also held on other important religious days such as the birthday of Prophet Mohammad or on the tenth day of *Muharram* (the lunar month of mourning) which is the anniversary of the massacre of Hazrat-e-Hussein, grandson of Mohammad and seventy-two members of his family. There is also *Nazer Bibi,* Bibi being Fatima El-Zahra, the daughter of Prophet Mohammad. On this occasion, rice or wheat *halwa* is served on round thin bread cooked in oil.

Of course, some traditions and customs have disappeared, especially in the cities. The towns and cities have become increasingly westernized, particularly the capital, Kabul. Tables and chairs are now in common use, as is cutlery, although knives are still not used much. Buffet meals are often prepared for large parties.

There is no special order for serving Afghan food and usually at a large party the table is set with all the main dishes; *pilau, qorma,* vegetables and salads are placed together with the desserts and fruits. It is up to the individual to choose whether to eat each dish separately or to eat all the dishes on one plate. However, the desserts are eaten last and followed by fruit. After every meal tea is served. Enormous amounts of food are prepared on special occasions. Second helpings are a must if you are not to offend your host. Often the host or hostess will come round and serve you with a large extra helping, insisting that you eat more of this or that delicacy.

Leftovers from these feasts are never wasted. There are always willing eaters in the kitchen who have been involved in the preparation of the food and who wait until the guests have finished. What they cannot manage can always be eaten the next day.

Afghans rarely eat in restaurants. There are a few restaurants in Kabul and in other large towns and these mostly cater to foreigners and travelers. *Chaikhana,* teahouses, on the other hand, are very popular and Afghans go there to meet their friends, exchange gossip and sit and drink tea. Food can be bought but it is mainly for travelers. Afghans do like to eat kebabs which are prepared at kebab stalls and they also buy snacks from street vendors known as *tawaf* or *tabang wala.* A *tabang wala* carries his food and utensils balanced on his head on a large, flat, round wooden tray called a *tabang.* He sets up a stall wherever or whenever appropriate, sometimes staking a claim to a particular street corner. He provides an assortment of food such as *jelabi, pakaura,* sliced boiled potatoes with vinegar, boiled chickpeas or kidney beans served with vinegar and boiled eggs.

A popular game played by children at *Eid* or *Nauroz* resembles our Easter custom of colored eggs. Eggs are brightly decorated in different colors and the game consists in knocking together two boiled eggs with a friend. The owner of the egg whose shell cracks first is the loser. Sometimes a *tabang wala* sells dried fruits and nuts, fruit and nut compotes such as *kishmish ab* (raisins in water), and sweets.

Another game that both adults and children play involves the pulling and breaking of a chicken wishbone. Very often at a party a *pilau* with chicken will be specially cooked as an excuse to play this game. Unlike the game played with a wishbone in the West, it does not matter who receives the larger piece; the pulling of the

Picnicking in the Hindu Kush.

wishbone simply marks the start of a game between two players, on which bets, usually for another party or money or clothing, will be placed. At any time after the wishbone has been pulled one of the players may try to win by handing an object, of any nature, to the other. The one who receives the object must remember that the game has been set in motion and must say *"Mara yod ast* (I remember)." The game goes on until one player forgets and becomes the loser. The winner marks his victory by saying *"Mara yod ast, tura feramush* (I remember, you forget)."

With the arrival of snow, the adults play a game called *barfi*, which also involves the giving of a party. A friend or relative sends a note in an envelope containing some of the first snow. It is usually delivered by a servant or a child. If you unsuspectingly accept the envelope you must pay the forfeit by giving a party for the sender and his family. Some Afghans take care to avoid answering the door during the first snowfall, but many will await the deliverer, for, if you can catch the person delivering the note, the tables are turned and it is the sender who must give the party. When this happens the deliverer has a black mark made with charcoal on his forehead or his hands are tied behind his back and then he is returned in disgrace to the sender's house. I was once caught by one of my husband's young cousins. I think his family took unfair advantage of a foreigner who was not well versed in Afghan traditions!

A favorite pastime is a picnic called *maila*, especially in spring and summer, although in peacetime the people of Kabul go for picnics even in winter, sometimes an extended one lasting the whole weekend, down in the warmer climes of Jalalabad. In summer, picnickers go to the cooler mountain regions of Paghman or the Salang in the Hindu Kush. In spring the picturesque village of Istalif and the lake at Sarobi are favorite haunts.

In true Afghan style, mountains of food are taken and prepared on the spot for these picnics. Kebabs or fish are grilled over charcoal and served with salads and hot fresh *nan*, bread. Sometimes the more adventurous cook *pilau*. Afterward tea is brewed and everyone relaxes and enjoys the fresh air. Some Afghan picnics are quite lively affairs, and there is music and dancing for the more energetic. People bring their own musical instruments, or popular Indian dance music on tape.

Some foods and desserts are prepared only in certain seasons. In spring or early summer, *faluda* is made. This is a type of noodle dessert or drink, sometimes mixed with snow brought down from the mountains in large blocks, which is served with a variety of accompaniments ranging from a milk custard thickened with salep to just being sprinkled with rosewater. Locally made ice cream, *sheer yakh,* may also be served. *Kishmish panir* is another traditional food found only in the spring: a white uncured cheese served with red raisins. Winter is the season for the speciality called *haleem,* a dish of wheat mixed with ground meat and served with oil and sugar, usually bought from the bazaar. Winter is also the time for fish and *jelabi.*

In the fish bazaar.

ABOUT THE RECIPES

These are based on my own experiences in Afghanistan, or have been given to me by Afghan friends and relatives. I have tested every one at home in England.

I could not include the recipes for all the known Afghan dishes. In making my choice, I have given preference to those which are most favored by Afghans and Westerners alike, and for which ingredients and utensils are readily available.

I have aimed throughout to give recipes in their authentic form, but some laborious and time-consuming procedures have been changed, and tips for shortcuts incorporated. Often these modifications have come from Afghans living in the West, who have had to make many adjustments and have worked out for themselves ways to maintain their own traditions successfully in a different environment. Where appropriate, I have suggested substitute ingredients.

Afghan cooks are not accustomed to using exact measures. I give such measures, without which many of the recipes would be puzzling to non-Afghans, but I don't mean them to be taken too literally. Especially with ingredients like salt, pepper, and cooking oil, amounts can be changed to suit individual tastes.

Although Afghans like to eat meat, many of the main dishes can be prepared without it and are suitable for vegetarians. Afghans themselves have had to adapt their diet in this way in times of shortage and hardship.

LANGUAGES

There are several languages in Afghanistan. The three main languages are Dari, which is closely related to the Farsi (Persian) spoken in Iran; Pashtu, which is the language of the Pashtuns; and Turkic, of which there are several different dialects. My Afghan family and most of my Afghan friends speak Dari, and this is also the language most commonly used in Kabul, so it was the one I learned. I give the names of dishes in a phonetic transcription of Dari, with apologies to language scholars for any inconsistencies.

An Afghan kitchen.

The
Afghan
Kitchen

The traditional Afghan kitchen is very basic. Few people have ovens, even in the cities. Most of the cooking is done over wood or charcoal fires, and many would say that Afghan food tastes much better if cooked thus. Some Afghans do, however, have a clay oven *(tandoor)*, used for baking their own bread.

Refrigerators are rare. To keep food cool and fresh in the hot summers, Afghans use a range of clay pots and containers shown in the drawings on page 19.

There is usually no running water. All washing up is done outside, using a well.

WEIGHTS AND MEASUREMENTS

Afghans rarely measure out their ingredients like people in western countries. Recipes tend to be passed down from mother to daughter and are learned through practice and experience. Most kitchens do, however, have a range of pots with handles called *malaqa,* which are used as measuring aids, and ordinary cups and glasses are also used for measuring.

Weights are used in buying food. Those used are the *seer, charak, pow, khord* and *misqal.* The last is the smallest and is used for weighing gold and spices. The approximate equivalences in the imperial system are as follows:

1 *seer* = 16 pounds
1 *charak* = ¼ *seer* = 4 pounds
1 *pow* = ¼ *charak* = 1 pound
1 *khord* = ¼ *pow* = 4 ounces
1 *misqal* = ½₄ *khord* = ⅒ ounce

I remember being amazed the first time I bought some fruit from a "donkey seller" (trader with a donkey, not selling donkeys) in the fruit bazaar. He took his hand scales and put the fruit on one end and a stone on the other! This stone represented 1 *pow.* Some foreigners who could not believe that they were being given the correct weight would rush to the nearest shop and ask them to weigh the goods with "proper" scales and weights. In fact, the hand scales were always accurate, but I never saw any of these poor donkey sellers getting annoyed or upset by this insult to their honesty. They would just smile and shrug their shoulders.

COOKS AND EQUIPMENT

Cooking is normally done by the female members of the family, although for big occasions and parties professional male cooks are hired. The men of the family are usually responsible for the shopping. Family is a much broader concept in the East. It does not refer only to immediate relatives. The size of the Asian extended family means that a large amount of food must be prepared each day and this takes considerable time.

Food tends to be cooked slowly so that the full flavors of the ingredients are brought out. Often a *pilau* will taste better warmed up the next day.

The methods of preparation are extensive and laborious, and sophisticated kitchen equipment such as electric food processors or grinders are practically nonexistent. However, most families do have a range of simple kitchen utensils and equipment. In the list which follows I indicate where more modern devices can be substituted.

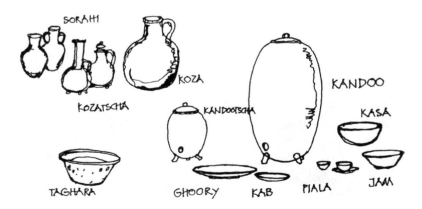

DAYG: pans

Afghan cooks use a collection of various copper pans, lined with an alloy which I believe contains zinc. Pans are named after the weight of rice which can be cooked in them. For example, *dayg-e-yak seera* is a pan used for cooking 1 seer (16 pounds) of rice. Pans range in size from just under 1 pound, *dayg-e-yak pow*, up to 10 seer (160 pounds), *dayg-e-dah seera*. Cast-iron pans are also used and recently aluminium pans have been introduced, but copper pans remain the most popular.

For cooking Afghan dishes, especially a *pilau*, I would recommend using heavy, thick-bottomed cast-iron pans, which prevent sticking and burning. It is also a good idea to have a heavy bottomed pan without a handle which can double up as a casserole for cooking in the oven. Pans in Afghanistan do not have handles and so can be used both on top of the stove and in the oven.

AWANG: pestle and mortar

All Afghan homes have a pestle and mortar, usually a brass one. They are essential for crushing garlic and onions and grinding herbs and spices. However, an electric grinder is a much quicker way of grinding spices, but take care to clean it after use. I sometimes use a garlic press for crushing garlic.

AWANG

MACHINE-E-GOSHT: mincer

Most Afghans possess their own mincer, as they mince their own meat for the preparation of *qima* (minced meat), *kofta* (meatballs) and some kebabs. They also use a mincer for shredding onions. To save time, a food processor can be used. In the old days in Afghanistan, before the modern mincer, meat was chopped up finely in the bazaar by the butcher, using a large chopper on a large wooden log.

KAFGEER: large slotted spoon

A long handled utensil used for stirring dishes and for serving rice. The head of a *kafgeer* is round, flat and slotted. An ordinary large slotted spoon makes a good substitute.

MALAQA: measuring pot

A range of pots with handles called *malaqa* are used for measuring out such things as flour, rice and liquids. Ordinary scales or weights can be used for the recipes in this book, along with a measuring jug for liquid measurements.

AUSH GAZ: rolling pin

To roll out dough for pasta dishes and some of their sweet pastries, Afghans use an *aush gaz*. This is a long, thin wooden stick, similar to a rolling pin.

CHALAU SOF: colander

A colander is used not only for washing and draining vegetables but for draining rice. *Chalau sof* literally means "drained white rice."

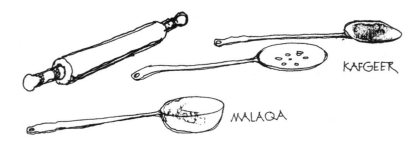

KAFGEER

MALAQA

DAYG-E-BOKHAR: steamer
This is the name for the steamer used for making the Uzbek dish of *mantu*. However, nowadays many Afghans possess pressure cookers and these are also called *dayg-e-bokhar*. *Bokhar* means "steam" in Dari.

MANQAL: barbecue (charcoal brazier)
For cooking small amounts of soup or frying eggs, or just for boiling water, many Afghans use a *manqal*. This is a small round iron device for cooking over charcoal, rather like a barbecue.

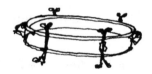

SIKH: skewers
Skewers are necessary for cooking some of the kebabs in this book. If you have a charcoal barbecue so much the better.

TAGHORA-E-KHAMIRI: mixing bowl
A large clay bowl used for kneading dough. An ordinary mixing bowl is perfectly adequate. Most Afghan kitchens also have a *taghora-e-qurooti*, the special bowl used for reconstituting *quroot*, strained and dried yogurt (page 40).

INGREDIENTS AND TECHNIQUES

Most of the ingredients used in this book can be bought without difficulty in supermarkets or delicatessens. Some are seasonal or more specialized but these can usually be found in Asian, Arab or Persian grocery shops.

Afghan food uses a wide variety of herbs and spices to add flavor and fragrance to dishes, with results which are neither too hot and spicy nor too bland. Spices and herbs are also valued by Afghans for their medicinal properties, many being used to aid the digestion or to help cure and alleviate other illnesses.

SPICES

Ideally spices should be bought whole and they will stay fresh for a long time if stored in cool, dry, dark places in tightly lidded jars. Spices can be ground with a pestle and mortar or in a grinder, such as an electric coffee grinder. Care must be taken that the grinder is thoroughly cleaned beforehand and afterwards so that no cross-flavoring occurs. One way to do this is to wipe the grinder out with kitchen paper and then grind one or two slices of stale bread.

It is also a good idea, if you use certain spices frequently, to use pepper mills for grinding them, one mill for each specific spice. I have a special one for grinding cardamom, which I use frequently in cooking and also, according to Afghan practice, for grinding cardamom into my tea.

Below I have listed alphabetically the spices most commonly used and which appear in the recipes in this book. The Afghan name is shown after the English one.

ANISE, ANISEED: *bodiyan*

Aniseed, *Pimpinella anisum*, an important spice in Afghanistan, is related botanically to caraway, cumin, dill and fennel. The seeds lend a lovely aromatic flavor to some baked goods such as savory biscuits and the bread called *roht*. Aniseed can also be used to flavor *qorma-e-Kashmiri*. The seeds are sometimes coated with sugar to make sweets called *noql* (see page 259), the same as the comfits which used to be made in Britain as an aid to digestion. Aniseed is still used as an aid to digestion in Afghanistan. It is often made into a sort of tea and given to babies to relieve gas and colic.

ASAFOETIDA: *hing*

I include this spice because, although it is rarely used in cooking in Afghanistan, large quantities are produced there, much of it for export, mainly to India where it is an important culinary spice.

Asafoetida is a dried gum resin which is obtained from the rhizome or taproots of some of the species of the giant fennels, plants of the genus *Ferula*, particularly *Ferula assafoetida*, which grows mainly in Afghanistan and Iran. The name asafoetida comes from the Persian word *aza* which means "mastic resin" and the Latin word *foetida* meaning "stinking." This name was no doubt given because of the spice's pungent and strong odor. One nickname given to asafoetida is "devil's dung."

The spice can be purchased in several forms; tears, lump, paste and powdered, the most common being the powdered or lump forms in the West.

In his *Account of the Kingdom of Caubul* of 1839, Mountstuart Elphinstone had the following to say about asafoetida:

> The assafoetida is found wild in the hills in many parts of the west. It requires no attention. It is a low bush with long leaves, which are generally cut off near the bottom of the stem; a milk exudes from the part cut, and gradually hardens like opium.

Although asafoetida is mainly used for medicinal purposes in Afghanistan it is still used in the preparation of *gosht-e-qagh*, dried meat. Fresh meat is sprinkled first with salt, then with powdered asafoetida, and then left to dry in the hot summer sun. This process helps prevent the meat from deteriorating or "going off." When required for cooking the dried meat is first soaked in water and then rinsed to remove the salt and asafoetida.

BLACK CUMIN SEED: (see NIGELLA and see also CUMIN)

CARDAMOM: *hail*

There are three types of cardamom used in Afghanistan: green, white and brown/black, according to the color of the pods containing the seeds, which constitute the spice. White cardamoms are simply green cardamoms which have been bleached. Green cardamoms are considered the best and are also known as true cardamom, *Elettaria cardamomum*. They are small oval-shaped pods containing black seeds that have a highly aromatic flavor. Brown cardamom of the genus *Amomum* are much larger, often with a ribbed or hairy skin and have a much stronger, camphor-like flavor. Green cardamoms, which are sometimes left whole, are used extensively in Afghanistan to flavor rice dishes, some *qormas*, desserts and in black or green tea. Brown cardamoms, because of their much stronger flavor are only used in small quantities in *char masala* (see FOUR SPICES) and in *pilaus*.

CASSIA: *dal chini*
    Dal chini is the name for both cassia (*Cinnamomum cassia*) and cinnamon (*C. zeylanicum*) in Afghanistan. Both come from the dried bark of trees in the laurel family. They have similar properties and can be used interchangeably as a flavoring in the kitchen. Cassia is sometimes used whole in stews and savory rice

Grinding spices.

dishes; but ground, it is mainly used in the spice mixture *char masala* (see FOUR SPICES). Cassia is sometimes known as Chinese cinnamon, whence *chini* in the Afghan name.

My first sight of cassia was when my cook in Kabul produced some coarse bits of bark in the kitchen. These smelled like cinnamon, but they looked quite different from the neat "quills" of cinnamon to which I was accustomed. My cook was equally baffled when I showed her a cinnamon stick—she had never seen that! I soon settled down to using cassia, as the Afghans do. It has a less intense aroma and flavor than cinnamon, but one can adjust quantities accordingly.

CHILIES: *murch-e-sabz, murch-e-surkh*

Chilies from the capsicum family, are "hot" and must be handled carefully—they contain an irritant, capsaicin, which can burn your skin, so always wash your hands after using them. We can now buy many varieties in the West and it can be quite difficult knowing which ones are really fiery, but in the Afghan kitchen they appear in just two main forms.

Murch-e-sabz are the long, fresh, green chilies. Afghans like to nibble these with their food, but they are also added whole to give flavor to soups and stews, or chopped and put in kebabs, salads, chutneys and pickles.

Murch-e-surkh are dried red chilies, to be used sparingly. They are sometimes added whole to soups and stews if a "hotter" flavor is required, but generally they are ground and become hot red pepper. They are rich in vitamins A and C.

CINNAMON: *dal chini*

Often confused with cassia in Afghanistan and they both bear the same name. Cinnamon, *Cinnamomum zeylanicum*, can be used interchangeably in Afghan dishes with cassia.

CILANTRO SEEDS: *tokhum-e-gashneez*

The seeds of the cilantro plant, *Coriandrum sativum*, form a spice, while its leaves are an herb. The seeds can be bought whole or ground and are used mainly for flavoring meatballs and stews. Their flavor is spicy and sweet, but mild.

CLOVES: *mikhak*
These are the dried flower buds of the shrub *Syzygium aromaticum*. The name comes from the Latin *clovus*, meaning nail; indeed *mikhak* also means "little nail" in Dari. Ground cloves are usually one of the spices in *char masala* (see FOUR SPICES), adding a rich, warm, "hot" aroma.

CUMIN: *zeera*
Cumin seeds have a strong, slightly bitter taste. In Afghan cookery they are either used whole or ground to flavor *pilaus* or *chalau*. They are also one of spices used in *char masala* (see FOUR SPICES). The seeds come from the dried fruits of *Cuminum cyminum*. *Zeeraee* in Dari means "dark brown" the color of the seeds. There is, however, a cumin that has black seeds called *sia zeera*, also prized in Afghanistan. *Sia zeera* are smaller and have a sweeter aroma than the brown variety. They should not be confused with NIGELLA (see page 28) which is often called "black cumin" (*sia dona*).

DILL SEED: *tokhum-e-shibit*
The seeds from the feathery herb, dill, are sometimes used as a substitute for aniseed (*bodiyan*).

FENUGREEK: *holba*
Fenugreek, *Trigonella foenum-graecum*, is favored in Afghanistan for its "hot" properties. It is often used to flavor spinach (which is considered "cold") and the sweet rice dish, *shola-e-holba*. The hard, yellow-brown seeds, rather like very small pebbles or stones, are rich in vitamins and have a strong, slightly bitter flavor. They are also used for some pickles such as *turshi limo* (lemon pickle).

FOUR SPICES: *char masala*
A similar concept to the *garam masala* of India and the Five Spice powder of China. The spices are ground and are used mainly to flavor *pilaus*. The choice of spices varies from family to family. Four commonly combined spices are cassia (or cinnamon), cloves, cumin and black cardamom seeds. Other spices sometimes combined include black pepper, green cardamom seeds and cilantro seeds.

GINGER: *zanjafeel*

Zanjafeel means "yellow elephant" and it is used both fresh and in powder form in Afghanistan. Ginger, *Zingiber officinale*, has a hot, lemony flavor and is considered good for colds, rheumatism, stomach complaints and indigestion. It is often used to flavor "windy" vegetables and pulse dishes, such as cauliflower and dal. A tea is also made with ginger. Ginger preserves are also popular.

NIGELLA: *sia dona*

These small black seeds, which can be bought under the name *kalonji* in an Asian grocery, are a confusing item because some people call them black onion seeds although they have nothing do with onions. They are also confused with caraway seeds. Another mistake is to call them black cumin seeds, as true cumin seeds come from a different plant. *Sia dona* come from the plant *Nigella sativa* and are sometimes called nigella seeds. The seeds have an earthy aroma and are often sprinkled on *nan* and savory biscuits before they are baked. They are also used in pickling. In this book I have used the Afghan name *sia dona*, which means "black seed."

PEPPER, BLACK: *murch-e-sia*

This is used liberally in many Afghan dishes.

PEPPER, RED: *murch-e-surkh*

Made from dried red chilies, this is usually called "red chili powder" by Asian grocers. It is like cayenne pepper. On the whole Afghan food is not very "hot," but some dishes benefit from a small amount.

POPPY SEED: *khoshkhosh*

Poppies, *Papaver somniferum*, grow abundantly in Afghanistan. Their seeds, whether white or black, are free from opium (as are the seeds of all poppies). They have a nutty flavor and are sometimes sprinkled on breads or savory biscuits.

SAFFRON: *zaffaron*

Saffron, which comes from the plant *Crocus sativus*, is a very expensive spice. It imparts a distinctive and highly aromatic flavor to many dishes, including *pilaus* and sweet dishes and also gives them a beautiful yellow-gold color. Although a little goes a long way, Afghans often substitute other colorings in their dishes. For example, turmeric is used in savory dishes such as *pilau* to colour the rice yellow. Afghans also use yellow food coloring which they call *rang-e-shireen*, literally "sweet color" for both savory and sweet dishes. Other ways of coloring *pilaus* are to add ground browned onions or caramelized sugar.

SESAME SEEDS: *dona-e-kunjid*
These have a lovely nutty flavor and are often sprinkled on breads before baking or ground to make sesame seed oil.

TURMERIC: *zard choba*
Closely related to ginger, from the rhizomes of *Curcuma longa*, turmeric is usually bought ground. It has a mild, earthy taste and is used for flavoring and to give a yellow color to *pilaus*, soups and stews. (*Zard* means "yellow" and *choba* means "wood.") It is never used to color desserts. Turmeric is considered to be good for digestion and liver ailments.

HERBS

CILANTRO: *gashneez*
This is my favorite herb although it is not liked by everybody, including my elder son, Alex. You either love it or hate it! It is used extensively in Afghanistan: in soups, stews, spinach, meatballs and salads. It can be stored successfully in the refrigerator if put in an airtight container in its unwashed state. The seeds are a spice.

DILL: *shibit*
This feathery herb, with a piquant flavor, is a member of the same family as parsley. Its licorice-like flavor is used in soups, some savory rice dishes and spinach. The seeds are a spice.

GARLIC: *seer*
Garlic is very popular, both as a flavoring and for medicinal purposes. It is said to tone up the digestive system. It is good for

marinating kebabs; is often added to soups, stews and vegetable dishes; and is also used in some pickles and chutneys.

MINT: *nahna*
Nahna is the common or garden mint. It is used both fresh and dried.

PENNYROYAL: *pudina*
Pudina, Mentha pulegium, is another popular flavoring, which often grows wild in Afghanistan. It is usually used in dried form, to be sprinkled over noodle and yogurt dishes such as *ashak*.

OTHER FLAVORINGS

ROSEWATER: *ab-e-gulab*
Rosewater has for long been used as a luxury flavoring (apart from its uses in medicine and as a perfume) in Afghanistan. It imparts a lovely delicate fragrance to special dishes for festive or religious occasions. It is considered "cold" according to the principles of *sardi/garmi* and it is often used to balance "hot" foods and dishes such as rich sweets or desserts. It is sometimes added to *pilaus* and refreshing shrub drinks.

The strength and sweetness of rosewater can vary considerably and it is best to buy rosewater from Asian, Persian or Middle Eastern stores. Even so, it is advisable to taste it for strength before using and adjust amounts accordingly. Always stir dishes containing rosewater with a wooden spoon. Metal ones will impart a metallic taste.

DISTILLATION OF ROSEWATER IN AFGHANISTAN

Afghanistan still follows the ancient method for distillating rosewater. My husband remembers his grandmother distilling rosewater in their garden when he was a little boy. The blooms were picked while very fresh in the cool, early hours of the morning. (It is usually the damask rose, *Rosa damascena*, which is used for making rosewater. This rose is sometimes called *gulab-e-asel*, meaning "original" rose.) The petals are picked off the blooms and piled up on a piece of cloth. A large copper pan or cauldron-type pot is then filled with water. The petals are added (the amount of water is usually about twice the weight of the petals).

Now the water is brought to a boil and a steady temperature is maintained; the boiling should not be too vigorous. The pot is covered with a type of copper dome to which is attached a pipe or tube. The apparatus is called an *ambiq*. The *ambiq* is joined by a pipe to a glass bottle called a *meena* (a poetical name that means "translucent"—the same word is often used in poetry to describe the sea or glass). The pipe fits inside the *meena* and is sealed with dough. The *ambiq* and the pot are also sealed with dough. This prevents the fragrant steam from escaping. The steam rises into the dome which is cooled by cold water, causing the steam to condense into droplets. The droplets travel along the pipe and slowly the fragrant rosewater drips into the bottle. Sometimes the rosewater from some or all of the bottles is poured into a larger pot or pan and slightly warmed again and left to stand until a thin film of oil forms on the surface. This is *atr* of roses; the Persian word, like the English version, attar, means "fragrant essence." It is collected by skimming it off with cotton wool and squeezing it into another smaller bottle.

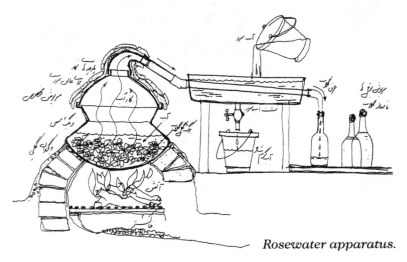

Rosewater apparatus.

Making rosewater in the garden.

PULSES

Many different kinds of pulses are used in Afghanistan; they help to provide protein and vitamin B especially when meat is not readily available. Apart from their food value, pulses are versatile and are used in many soups, and rice and meat dishes.

All pulses should be picked over and washed. Whole beans should be soaked overnight in water before cooking. Cooking time depends on the freshness of the pulses; fresh pulses cook more quickly. The best time to add salt is halfway through the cooking time or at the end, as salt tends to slow down the softening.

Below I have listed those pulses which are regularly used in Afghan dishes and can be obtained easily.

CHICKPEAS: *nakhud*

Chickpeas are used in a number of dishes, especially in soups such as *aush* and *maushawa* but they are also the main ingredient in the street food, *shour nakhud*. They also play a major part in the winter rice dish, *mastawa*.

MUNG BEANS: *maush*

Mung beans are small, green, oval shaped beans used to make bean sprouts in Oriental cooking. In Afghanistan they are used in short-grain rice dishes such as *ketcheree quroot* and *shola goshti* and also in the soup *maushawa*. If you cannot find them, substitute green lentils.

RED KIDNEY BEANS: *lobiya*

These are large, dark red kidney-shaped beans. They are used in soups and meat dishes.

SPLIT PEAS: *dal nakhud*

Yellow split peas are popular. Apart from being added to soups and stews they are often ground in meat patties such as *shami kebab* and are an essential ingredient of *do piaza*. When cooking these peas, leave the lid slightly ajar to prevent the thick froth that forms during cooking from boiling over. The froth should be skimmed off.

MOONG DAL: *dal*

This *dal* is the skinned and split version of the green mung beans used in dishes such as *maushawa* and *shola*. The grains are pale yellow and slightly elongated. The word *dal* applies to both the split beans and to the dish made with them.

VEGETABLES

ONIONS: *piaz*

Onions play an important role in Afghan cookery, and two types are used, red and white. The red onions are preferred for cooking as they give a thicker sauce and a richer flavor. The white onions are more commonly used in salads.

It is important that onions are fried properly. Use plenty of oil and start the frying on a medium to high heat, turning it down a little as the onions begin to brown, lose water and become soft. If the onions are fried over too high a heat they will brown too quickly and will not dissolve. They will also impart a slightly bitter taste and the sauce will not thicken properly. Afghans use plenty of onions to make their stews and sauces thick and rich.

Scallions, *noash piaz*, are not only eaten with salads but often make a tasty snack, sprinkled with salt and eaten with fresh *nan*.

GANDANA

I used to refer to this as Chinese chives, which are indeed very similar. But the most up-to-date and authoritative source I have consulted, *Cornucopia*, second revised edition (written by Stephen Facciola), identifies *gandana* as a cultivar of *Allium ampeloprasum* and also observes that another cultivar of that species, *tarreh Irani* (also known as Persian chives) is identical to this or nearly so.

Gandana is a very popular vegetable/herb in Afghanistan. The leaves are long and flat, looking rather like long grass. They have a sort of oniony/garlic flavor and they are used in a number of dishes such as *ashak,* in the tasty snack *boulanee* and to flavor spinach. Unless you grow your own, *gandana* may be difficult to obtain, so leeks (which have a similar taste) may be used, although some people prefer to substitute spring onions (scallions). A combination of both is also possible.

TOMATOES: *bonjon-e-rumi*
Tomatoes are used to flavor and color meat dishes and soups and of course they are eaten raw on their own and in salads. In the summer months, when tomatoes are cheap and plentiful, tomato paste and chutneys are made at home for use during the winter months.

EGGPLANT: *bonjon-e-sia*
Eggplants are widely used and play an important part in the Afghan diet. They are cooked in various ways. I have noticed that eggplants are rarely bitter, so I no longer recommend salting before use. Small "baby" eggplants are often made into pickles.

RADISHES: *mooli safaid, mooli surkh*
There are two main kinds of radish in Afghanistan. We are all familiar with the small red ones, *mooli surkh*, with their slightly peppery taste. They are eaten raw and in salads in Afghanistan, often chopped and mixed with other ingredients. *Mooli safaid*, the long white radish, *Raphanus sativus*, is known as daikon in China and Japan. This radish which usually has a muted peppery taste is also eaten raw and in salads and is also sometimes used in fish stews.

PUMPKINS, SQUASHES, GOURDS AND MARROWS
These all belong to the Cucurbit family and, confusingly, they are usually all lumped together under the Persian name *kadu* in Afghanistan. Some Afghans, however, call marrow and gourds *turaie*. *Turi* or *tarra* is the name given to the long, thin vegetable called luffa (*Luffa acutangula*).

FRUITS AND NUTS

Some fruits deserve special mention because they are not so well known and others because they are often used in Afghan cuisine.

APRICOTS: *zard olu*
Zard olu literally means "yellow, round fruit." They are sometimes added to *qorma* and *pilau,* adding not only color but giving

a sweet-sour taste often favored by Afghans. The dried small, white and very sweet apricots called *shakar paura* are often used in the traditional fruit compote, *Haft miwa*. The Hunza apricots we can now find in health food stores look very similar although I find that they do not have the same sweetness. Another variety of apricot called *quaysee*, is white, larger in size and has a pinkish blush. The Panjshir valley is particularly noted for its apricot trees. Apricot kernels called *khastah* are often used as a substitute for almonds.

CHERRIES: *gilas* and *olu bolu*

There are two kinds of cherries in Afghanistan: the sweet cherry, *gilas*, and the sour cherry, *olu bolu*. The sweet one, which is usually red, is enjoyed as a dessert fruit. The sour cherry which is larger and very dark red, almost black, with a dark red flesh, is preferred for the slightly bitter flavor it imparts when used in stews, rice dishes, chutney, beverages and jams. These cherries are often dried.

GRAPES: *angoor*

There are many varieties of grapes grown in regions all over Afghanistan. There are small, sweet white ones (*kishmishi*); round, green plump ones (*ghola don*); long, very sweet, pale green ones (*Husseini*); small red juicy ones; and big round or oval reddish-purple ones (*Kandahari*). Many are sent for export. They are a frequent addition to the fruit bowl in the summer and autumn and are usually served as a dessert after food, although they can be served as a refreshing snack at any time of the day.

A tart, slightly sour flavoring called *ghooray angoor* is made from small, young, sour green grapes. These are dried in the sun, then ground. This is used in mainly to flavor fish dishes such as *kebab-e-daygi-e-mahi*. Grapes seeds are crushed to be sprinkled over kebabs.

When there is a glut of grapes, a juice or syrup is made called *sheera-e-angoor*. The syrup is spread on bread (*nan*), rather like a jam. Vinegar (*sirka*) is also made from grapes. Grapes are dried to provide both green and red RAISINS (see below) for which Afghanistan is famous.

MELON/WATERMELON: *kharbusa/tarbuz*

Melons are another fruit for which Afghanistan is renowned. As long ago as the ninth century, Arab accounts relate how melons were packed in snow inside lead molds and sent to grace the table of the caliph of Baghdad.

As with grapes, there are numerous varieties. It was a common sight in the warm summer and autumn evenings to see melon stalls by the roadside. People would pick up a melon on their way from work to take home to their families.

The flesh of the melon, after the rind is removed, is sometimes used fresh or dried in *pilaus*. A speciality of the region Maimana in the north of Afghanistan, is *qandak-e-Maimana*, a *qorma* made from dried melon.

Watermelons are also very popular, especially in the hot summer months and the seeds are dried, which then make a tasty snack.

MULBERRIES, WHITE AND BLACK: *tut, shah tut*

Mulberry trees abound in Afghanistan, and were probably introduced there from China along the Silk Road. Both kinds of mulberry trees, *Morus alba* and *Morus nigra* (white and black mulberry respectively) are cultivated. They are known as *tut* and *shah tut*, *shah* meaning "king" and *tut*, "mulberry." They are cultivated primarily for their leaves for feeding silkworms but mulberries also play a substantial role in the Afghan diet. Afghans not only eat fresh mulberries in season but, more important, they dry them. Dried mulberries are mixed with ground walnuts making a combination called *chakida*. It is a highly nutritious food, providing nourishment for long journeys or supplementing the diet in winter. Another mulberry product is *talkhun*. This is mentioned by Eric Newby in his book, *A Short Walk in the Hindu Kush*. *Talkhun* is a kind of bread made with dried ground mulberries mixed with roasted flour or cornstarch. Sometimes the mixture is cooked with extra water to make a paste. This is then served in a mound on a plate, a well is made in the center and hot oil is added. *Sheer-e-tut*, which means "mulberry milk," is also sometimes made by steeping dried mulberries in water overnight, although the fresh fruit may sometimes be made into a beverage.

BOKHARA PLUM: *Olu Bokhara*

Bokhara plum, *Prunus bokhariensis*, are often used in Persian and Central Asian cuisines. When fresh they are golden in color but they are bought dried for use in cooking and lend an unusual, slightly tart flavor to a number of dishes. They can usually be found in Persian shops. Prunes make an acceptable substitute. There are several varieties of plum to be found in Afghanistan. One is a small green *olucha*, which appears in spring. Another is *gurdolu*, a large purple plum.

QUINCE: *behi*

The quince, *Cydonia oblonga*, a relative of the apple and pear, originated in the Caucasus. It is still appreciated there and in other countries of the region, including Afghanistan, for the scent and sweet/sour flavor it imparts to sauces and stews. The quince, when cooked, becomes a lovely pink color and it is this color along with its delicate fragrance that makes it a favorite fruit with Afghans for making compotes, jams and shrubs.

POMEGRANATE: *anar*

Pomegranates are a popular fruit in Afghanistan. The Kandahar region and the Konar region are particularly famous for this fruit. The seeds, *anar dona*, are often eaten in the same way I remember from my childhood in England: with a special needle. Many Afghans serve the seeds in a small bowl and then sprinkle them with black pepper. The juice is extracted from the seeds to make a refreshing drink. The seeds are also used in medicine.

RAISINS: *kishmish*

The main types of raisins in Afghanistan are: *kishmish surkh* (red raisins). *kishmish sabz* (green raisins), *monaqa* or *kishmish sia* (large black raisins with seeds) and *zereshk-e-shireen* (a currant). *Zereshk* is also the name given to the barberry, which is used in cooking in the region of Herat, but is more well known in Iran, especially for its use in their famous *Zereshk pilau*.

A common sight driving along the long roads of Afghanistan, especially in the Koh Daman region, north of Kabul are houses with extended double-storied rooms with slotted walls for producing raisins. Nancy Dupree in her *An Historical Guide to Afghanistan* gives a good description:

> The Koh Daman is most famous perhaps for its grapes and vineyards, which proliferate as you proceed toward the head of the valley. You will note that many houses have extended double-storied rooms with slotted walls. Called *sayagi-khana* these rooms contain a network of long poles from floor to ceiling which are festooned with bunches of fresh grapes. The slotted walls allow air to circulate through the fruit, turning the grapes into green raisins.
>
> During the harvest from about August through October you may also observe grapes laid out to dry in large stone-ringed plots beside the black goats' hair and white cloth tents of nomads who come to the valley to assist in the harvest. These sun-dried raisins turn a dark red. Some of the choicest varieties, such as the olive-shaped Hussaini, are carefully packed in cotton wool in small shaved-wood boxes or sealed between two clay plates and sold as a delicacy during the winter months.

NUTS: *Khastah*

Almonds (*badom*), pistachios (*pistah*), pine nuts (*jalghroza*), walnuts (*charmaghz*, which interestingly means "four brains", a name given because of its resemblance to a brain) are all used extensively either whole, slivered, chopped or ground in Afghan *pilaus*, pastries and desserts. They are also eaten on their own as snacks, often salted and mixed with dried fruits such as raisins and served with tea. Herat is particularly noted for its good pistachios as is the north of Kabul for walnuts.

OTHER INGREDIENTS

VEGETABLE OIL: *roghan-e-naboti*

Traditionally Afghans cooked with what is called *roghan-e-dumbah*, a fat rendered from the tail of the fat-tailed sheep and *roghan-e-zard*, a clarified butter, often called ghee (as in India). *Roghan-e-dumbah* is cheaper but *roghan-e-zard* is more readily available and popular. Vegetable shortening and vegetable oil are also used. Two factories at Lashkargah and Kunduz produce edible cotton seed vegetable oil.

I have used vegetable oil for the recipes in this book. Corn oil and sunflower oil are both suitable.

Afghan tastes favor a large amount of fat or oil; indeed, this is also a sort of status symbol. If you are wealthy you can afford more cooking oil. I have taken western tastes into account while preparing the recipes, but the amount of oil or fat used can be further adjusted; and any unwanted oil can always be spooned off just before serving.

YOGURT: *mast*

A lot of live, natural yogurt (i.e. containing cultures) is eaten and is also used in Afghan cooking. It is often strained to make a thick creamy substance called *chaka*, which is made by draining the yogurt in a cheesecloth or muslin bag for about an hour. *Chaka* is preferred for use in cooking because it avoids imparting any acid or sour taste which the whey in ordinary yogurt can give to a dish. Greek-strained yogurt has much the same properties.

DRIED YOGURT: *quroot*

Chaka is often salted and dried and formed into round balls, called *quroot*. They look rather like white pebbles and are quite hard. For use in cooking they are reconstituted in water in a special bowl called a *taghora qurooti*. This clay bowl has small pebbles embedded in its base giving a rough, uneven surface for the *quroot* to be rubbed against thus helping to break them up. Afghans sometimes add to the plain reconstituted *quroot* some garlic, salt and pepper, then boil it all and eat it with *nan*. For added flavor they sprinkle dried mint on top. This dish, called *qurooti*, was a favorite of my mother-in-law, who would potter into the kitchen and make it for herself whenever she fancied some, which was quite often.

CLOTTED CREAM: *qymaq*

Qymaq is a milk product which has some resemblance to clotted cream and is clearly a close relation of the *kaymak* of the

Draining yogurt to make chaka.

Middle East. It can be bought from dairy shops in Afghanistan or prepared at home. *Qymaq* can be made from the milk of water buffalo, cows or goats, that of the water buffalo making a much thicker, creamier version. A bowl of *qymaq* with *nan* is often enjoyed for breakfast, or it is served with fruit compotes, but it is better known in *qymaq chai*, a green tea prepared in a special way with *qymaq* floating on top.

SALEP: *Sahlab*

Sahlab is a fine white powder obtained from the dried root tubers of some orchids, especially *Orchis latifolia*. It is used in many parts of the Middle East in ice creams and to thicken milk drinks. In Afghanistan it is also used to thicken milk to make a sort of custard which is often served with *faluda* or added to ice cream mixtures, giving a lovely texture and elasticity. It is considered a strengthening food.

"HOT" AND "COLD" FOOD

Many people in Afghanistan still adhere in everyday life to the ancient Persian concept of *sardi/garmi*, literally cold/hot. Like "yin-yang" in China, it is a system for classifying foods for the purpose of dietary health. People believe that by eating "hot" foods, "cold" illnesses such as the common cold or depression can be alleviated. "Cold" foods are prescribed to reduce fevers or hot tempers! "Hot" and "cold" here refer to the properties of the food, not the temperature.

Most of us practice something like this quite unwittingly in our own homes by eating what is known as a balanced diet. In winter we eat foods which are "hotter" such as stews and thick soups. In summer we eat more salads, fruits and lighter dishes.

While not everyone would agree on the details of classifying foods as "hot" or "cold" there is a definite pattern. "Hot" foods in general are rich, warm in aroma, sweet and high in calories and carbohydrates. "Cold" foods on the other hand are generally characterized by acidity or are bland, have a high water content and are low in calories. These are some examples of what are considered "hot" and "cold" foods in Afghanistan:

- "Hot" foods include sugar and honey; fats and oils; wheat flour and chickpea flour; dried fruits such as raisins and mulberries; nuts such as almonds and pistachios; garlic and onions; fish; meats such as beef and lamb and game meats such as duck, pigeon and partridge; eggs; and most spices such as chilies, fenugreek, ginger, turmeric and saffron.

- "Cold" foods include rosewater; milk and yogurt; rice; fresh fruits such as melon, peaches, grapes, pears, apples and lemon; vegetables such as spinach, cucumber, lettuce, and some pulses such as lentils and kidney beans; chicken; and most herbs such as cilantro and dill.

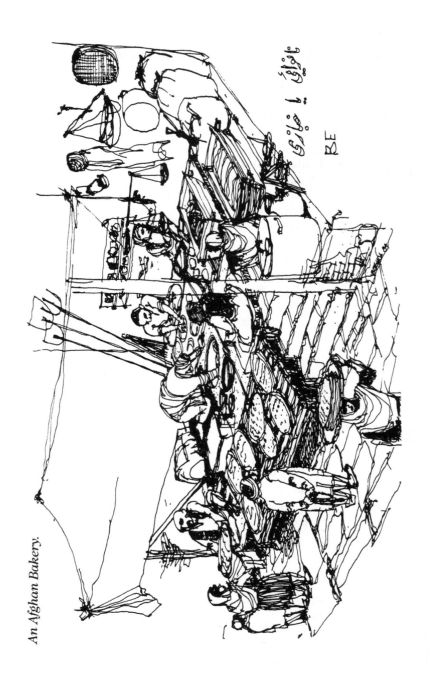

An Afghan Bakery.

Breads

*N*an, bread, and *chai*, tea, are the basic diet of all Afghans. The word *nan* actually means "food" in Afghanistan. The bread is nutritious as well as delicious. The size and shape vary in different parts of the country.

Regular *nan* is made of whole-wheat flour and is leavened with a fermented starter prepared from a small lump of the dough from the previous day. This will have been left in a warm place overnight. It is called *khamir tursh* (sour dough).

Most families make their own bread fresh every day and either bake it in their own *tandoor* or take the dough to the local *tandoor* bakery, known as the *nanwaee*. A *tandoor* is a clay oven built into the ground which is capable of reaching temperatures far higher than an ordinary domestic oven. The bread is cooked by flattening the dough against the hot inner wall.

Our family did not have its own *tandoor* so my servant used to prepare the dough first thing in the morning and leave it to rise in a sunny place for an hour or so. Then she would form the dough into round balls of equal size and carry these on her head, balanced on a large tray made from woven straw (*tukri nan*), to the *nanwaee*. The dough would be left there to be baked and she would collect the breads later on, usually in time for lunch. The number of breads baked for us each day would be notched on a long stick called a *chobe khat*. At the end of the week the number of notches were added up so that we could pay our bill. It was of course possible to buy *nan* which was both prepared and baked at the *nanwaee*.

Breads are also cooked on a *tawah*. This is a curved, circular cast-iron plate which is heated before the bread is slapped onto it. As the plate is portable this method is especially used by the nomads of Afghanistan. The bread cooked on a *tawah* is unleavened and known as *chapati* or *nan-e-tawagi*.

Lawausha is another popular bread which is similar in size and shape to *chapati* but is leavened and baked in a *tandoor*.

Uzbek bread, often baked in special Uzbek ovens, is more commonly found in the north of Afghanistan.

A tasty bread called *nan-e-tomarch* (sometimes known as *nan-e-gigeqi*), which is especially popular in the north of Afghanistan, is made by rendering the fat (*dumba*) from the tail of the fat-tailed sheep. The *dumba* is cut into small pieces and fried until only the crispy fat remains. This is called *gigeq*. The *gigeq* is then ground and mixed into bread dough. The breads are sprinkled with *sia dona* (nigella seeds) and baked.

I should mention two other breads, which are often served for breakfast or with tea. *Nan-e-roghani* contains some oil but is basically the same as regular *nan*. *Roht* is a sweet bread containing sugar, milk and fat.

Bread is eaten with most meals in Afghanistan and with the right hand. It is used to soak up soup, to scoop up food or for eating with rice and kebabs.

Afghans use finely ground whole-wheat flour for most of their bread but the whole-wheat flour found in the West is too coarse so I have substituted *chapati* or *ata* flour, which can be bought at Asian grocers. The closest U.S. equivalent is "bread flour."

The bread dough must be quite soft and the amount of water you use to form it will depend on the type of flour and the humidity of the air. Adjust the quantity of water suggested in the recipe as necessary. Because the dough is soft, the breads need to be patted or rolled out with a fair amount of extra flour.

NAN
Bread

Nan is a leavened bread, made with *khamir tursh*, a sourdough starter. Dried yeast can be used for leavening, as in the recipe below, but the flavor is not quite the same. The method of baking in a *tandoor* oven at very high temperature also contributes to the flavor. *Nan* can, however, be baked satisfactorily in an ordinary oven, if preheated to the highest setting. It is best eaten straight from the oven, still warm, although it can be served cold. One way of "freshening up" the bread, if it has gone cold or has been taken from the freezer, is to sprinkle it with a little water on both sides and quickly warm it up under a hot broiler.

It can be cut into small pieces or served whole. Traditionally, *nan* is served with every meal and eaten without butter. It is, however, also delicious with butter, and perhaps even cheese or jam, as a snack.

    1½ lbs (5¼ cups) *chapati* flour
    1½ tsp salt
    1 pkt quick rising yeast
    4-5 tsp vegetable oil (optional)
    2 cups warm water
    sia dona (nigella seeds), poppy seeds, sesame seeds (optional)

Sift the flour with the salt into a bowl. Add the yeast and mix to combine the dry ingredients. Mix in the vegetable oil and rub in with the hands. Gradually add the warm water to the flour and yeast and mix with the hands until a smooth, round, soft dough is produced. Knead for another 7 to 10 minutes until the dough is elastic and smooth, essentially the same as ordinary bread dough. Form into a ball, cover with a damp cloth and leave to rest in a moderately warm place for about an hour or until the dough has doubled in bulk.

Preheat the oven to 500°F. Line a baking tray with aluminium foil and place in the oven to get hot.

When the dough has risen divide into four equal sized balls. Shape or roll out on a lightly floured surface into oval shapes to a thickness of about ½ inch. After shaping the *nan*, wet your hand and form deep grooves down the center of each. In Afghanistan the grooves are made with either fingers or thumb or a special cutter and this depends on whether the baker is a woman or a man.

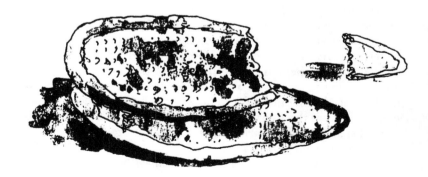

Cuts are made by men, grooves by women. Sprinkle lightly with the *sia dona* or poppy or sesame seeds if wished.

Remove the hot baking tray from the oven and place a *nan* onto it. Bake immediately for 8 to 10 minutes until the *nan* is golden brown. The bread should be fairly crisp and hard on the outside. Repeat the process with the remaining balls of dough.

When removed from the oven the *nan* should be wrapped in a clean tea towel or tin foil to prevent drying out.

MAKES 4

 **LAWAUSHA**

To make *lawausha*, prepare the dough as for *nan*, but roll out to a larger, thinner size. For 1½ lbs flour you may need to divide the dough into six in order to fit them on to a baking sheet. No grooves or cuts are made on *lawausha* and they are not decorated in any way. The cooking time will be less. Very good breads similar to *lawausha* can be purchased from Arab shops or bakeries.

MAKES 4 BREADS

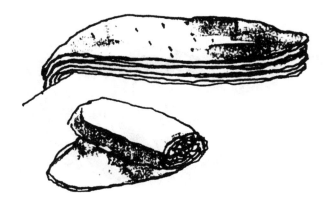

NAN-E-UZBEKI

My parents came to visit me in Afghanistan several times and one of their outstanding memories was of the tour we made to the north of Afghanistan. We traveled over the lofty peaks of the Salang Pass on the twisting mountain rounds, through the Salang tunnel at an elevation of 12,000 ft. to visit Kunduz, Tashkurgan, Mazar-e-Sharif and Balkh. It was in Tashkurgan, the town with its famous covered bazaar, that they were introduced to the delicious local *nan-e-Uzbeki*.

This is a round, flat bread found mainly in the north of Afghanistan. It is similar to ordinary *nan*, except that it is round in shape, is slightly thicker, especially round the edges, and is usually glazed with milk or egg. It is also stamped or pressed with a special wooden implement to make intricate designs before being baked. The wooden stem or base has wires or nails driven into it to form a pattern. The patterns or designs vary considerably. The baker holds the wooden stem in his hand and presses the nails into the bread to form designs before baking it. The bread is then glazed and often further decorated by sprinkling with sesame seeds, poppy seeds or black cumin seeds.

To make *nan-e-Uzbeki*, prepare the dough as for *nan*, but roll out and prepare as described above, substituting a fork for the implement described above to make patterns.

MAKES **4** BREADS

 NAN-E-ROGHANI

Nan-e-roghani is basically *nan*, except that it contains oil or fat and is usually served with tea for breakfast or in the afternoon. This bread is usually brushed with an egg glaze before baking and sprinkled with *sia dona* (see p. 28), sesame seeds or poppy seeds.

1½ lbs (5¼ cups) *chapati* flour
1½ tsp salt
1 pkt quick rising yeast
3 tbs vegetable oil
2 cups warm water
beaten egg for glazing
sia dona (nigella seeds), poppy seeds or sesame seeds

Sift the flour with the salt into a bowl. Add the yeast and mix into the dry ingredients. Mix the oil and warm water together and gradually add to the dry ingredients, mixing well together with the hands. Knead until a round, soft dough is produced. Knead for a further 7 to 10 minutes until the dough is elastic and smooth. Form into a ball, cover with a damp cloth and leave to rest in a moderately warm place for about an hour or until the dough has doubled in bulk.

Preheat the oven to 500°F. Brush the baking tray(s) lightly with oil. Divide the dough into four and roll out into oval shapes about 10 inches by 6 inches. Either prick all over with a fork or prepare as for *nan*, by wetting your hands with water and forming deep grooves down the center of each. Brush with the egg glaze and sprinkle with the chosen seeds. Place the *nan* on to the baking tray(s) and put in the hot oven. Bake for about 5 minutes, then reduce the heat to 425°F and cook for a further 5 to 10 minutes or until lightly browned. Turn the breads over and bake for a few more minutes until the underside is brown.

When the breads are removed from the oven you may sprinkle them with a little water before covering with a clean cloth or wrapping in tin foil. This helps keep the bread moist and soft until ready to eat.

MAKES 4 BREADS

VARIATION:

Nan-e-maghzi is a similar bread with the addition of milk. Instead of 2 cups of warm water use a mixture of 1¼ cups warm water and ¾ cup warm milk.

 **CHAPATI**

Flat Bread

These are best eaten hot and freshly made and are usually served with kebabs and meat dishes such as *do piaza*.

8 ounces (1¾ cups) *chapati* flour
½ tsp salt

Sift the flour with the salt into a bowl and slowly add ½ to ¾ cup of water, mixing with the hand, to form a soft dough. Knead for 7 to 10 minutes until the dough is smooth. Cover with a damp cloth and set aside for an hour.

Heat a large cast-iron frying pan (which serves well instead of the traditional *tawah* described on p. 46) over a medium heat. Divide the dough into 8 pieces and form into round balls. Roll out each ball, using a little extra flour; until it is quite thin and 7 to 8 inches in diameter. (Afghans usually make larger; oval shapes, but the size recommended fits a frying pan better.) Pick up each *chapati* in turn between two hands and pat it gently to shake off excess flour; then slap it onto the hot pan. Cook for about 1 minute, then turn over and cook for about another minute. As you cook, press down the edges gently with tongs, so as to cook evenly. The *chapati* should puff up. As each is done, put it on a dish, covered with a towel to keep warm.

MAKES 8

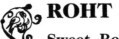 ROHT
Sweet, Round Flat Bread

Roht is a slightly sweet and moist bread which is enjoyed with tea or hot milk at breakfasttime. It is also traditionally made for the festivities when a newborn child is forty days old. This recipe was given to me by my friend, Aziza Ashraf.

1½ lbs (5¼ cups) all-purpose flour
2 level tsp baking powder
1 pkg quick rise yeast
¼ tsp ground cardamom
¾ cup vegetable oil
1½ cups sugar
¾ cup warm water
1 egg, beaten
1 level tbs yogurt
sia dona (nigella seeds)
sesame seeds

Mix together the flour, baking powder, yeast and cardamom.

Warm the oil in a small pan, then add to the flour and rub together for a few minutes. Add the sugar to the warm water and gradually add to the flour, mixing well. Now add the egg (reserving a little for glazing) and the yogurt. Mix well and knead into a quite soft dough for about 5 minutes. Cover with a cloth and leave in a warm place for about an hour or so.

Meanwhile preheat the oven to 425°F.

Divide the dough into two and roll out each on a floured surface into a round of about ½-inch thickness. Prick all over with a fork, glaze with the reserved egg and sprinkle the top with the *sia dona* and sesame seeds according to your fancy.

Place on a slightly oiled or greased baking tray and bake in the hot oven for about 15 minutes until risen, golden brown and cooked through. (If the top is browning too quickly turn down the heat and cook on the lower heat for a little longer.)

Remove from the oven and place in a warm tea towel or plastic bag to stop the bread drying out too much.

MAKES **2** BREADS

Soups

Soup, *sherwa*, is one of the basic foods of Afghanistan. *Sherwa* comes from the Persian word *shorba*, *shor* meaning "salty" and *ba* meaning "stew, dish cooked with water." Most Afghan soups are quite substantial and are often prepared as a main meal. Many of them contain meat and or pulses of some kind. Eaten with *nan* they make a nourishing and filling meal. The usual way is to break up the *nan* into the soup to soak and then to eat it either with the hand or with a spoon.

Sherwa-e-tarkari is perhaps the most common, made with meat and vegetables, but the ingredients vary according to what is available. It is quite usual for fresh cilantro to be added as it lends such a delicious flavor to the soup. Perhaps the most traditional soup of Afghanistan and the most unusual, is the *sherwa-e-chainaki* which means "teapot soup," and this soup is literally made in a teapot.

SHERWA-E-TARKARI
Meat and Vegetable Soup

This soup is very common and there are no hard and fast rules. There are many versions and ingredients vary according to what vegetables are available. Lamb, beef or chicken may be used for the meat.

> 6 tbs vegetable oil
> 2 medium onions, chopped
> 1 lb meat on the bone
> 1 can (8 ounces) tomatoes
> salt and pepper
> 8 oz potatoes, peeled and cut into small pieces (about 1½ cups)
> 4 oz carrots, scraped and cubed (about ½ cup)
> 2 oz fresh cilantro

Heat the oil in a large pan and fry the onions over a medium to high heat until golden brown and soft. Add the meat and continue frying until the meat is brown all over. Add the tomatoes, salt, pepper and 3 to 4 cups of water. Bring to a boil, then turn down the heat and simmer until the meat is almost cooked about 1 to 1½ hours depending on the type of meat cooked. Now add the potatoes and carrots and cook for a further 20 to 30 minutes or until the vegetables are cooked. Wash the cilantro and remove the stalks and then add to the soup. Cook for a further 5 minutes or so, adding a little more water if required.

This soup is always served with a fresh *nan* or *chapati*.

SERVES 4

SHERWA-E-SHAMALI-WAR
"Hot" Meat and Vegetable Soup

This soup comes from the north of Kabul; its name translates to mean "soup of the northerners." It is renowned for its hot and spicy flavor.

½ cup vegetable oil
2 to 3 medium onions, sliced thinly
2 cloves garlic, peeled and crushed
1½ lbs meat on the bone, preferably lamb
2 oz split peas
1 can (14 oz) chopped tomatoes
1 or 2 hot red or green chilies, or more, according to taste
2 tsp ground cilantro
1 to 2 tsp turmeric
1 to 2 tsp ground black pepper
3 to 4 medium potatoes, peeled and cut into cubes
4 oz fresh cilantro leaves
salt

Heat the oil in a large pan and fry the onions over a medium to high heat until golden brown and soft. Add the garlic and the meat and continue frying until the meat is brown all over. Add the split peas, tomatoes, chilies and spices and then about 6 or 7 cups of water. Bring to a boil, turn down the heat and simmer until the meat is almost cooked, about 1¼ hours. Then add the potatoes and fresh cilantro, and simmer for a further 20 to 30 minutes or until the potatoes are soft. If the liquid has reduced too much, add extra water. Add salt.

This soup is served with fresh *nan* or *chapati* with a side dish of sliced onions marinated in vinegar, or a mixed salad.

SERVES 6

SHERWA-E-CHAINAKI
Teapot Soup

This is the most traditional soup served in *chaikhanas* all over Afghanistan. It is very simple and basic but quite delicious and is made, as the name implies, in a teapot! The sort of teapots used are broken teapots which have been mended by someone called a *patragar* "a person who mends." He sits cross-legged and holds the broken pieces of teapot (which are held together with string) with his feet. Then with a drill, which is pointed with an ordinary gramophone needle, he pierces holes in the pottery. He clips the pieces of pottery together with pieces of wire and then seals all the mends with a mixture of egg white and gypsum and leaves it to dry and harden.

To make the soup all the ingredients are placed in the teapot, the lid replaced and then the whole teapot is placed among the hot embers raked from either a charcoal brazier which has been used for making kebabs or from the fire beneath the boiling samovar.

This soup is usually made early in the morning and left to simmer slowly among the burning embers until lunchtime. When the customer orders his soup, he is served with the teapot containing the soup, a bowl and one large *nan*. He then breaks up some of the *nan* into pieces and adds them to the bowl. The soup is poured over the *nan* which soaks up the juices. The soaked *nan* is then scooped up either by hand or with a spoon.

The recipe I give below is adapted for use in a kitchen.

1 small onion, finely chopped or sliced
2 small portions of lamb on the bone with some fat (about 4 oz)
1 tbs split peas
1 tbs chopped fresh cilantro
salt and pepper to taste

Place the onion, lamb and peas into a small pot or pan. Add enough water to cover. Slowly bring to a boil then turn down the heat, cover with a lid and leave to simmer for 1 to 2 hours. Just before serving add the cilantro and adjust the seasoning, if required.

Serve with *nan* or bread and perhaps a side salad of sliced onions dressed in a little white wine vinegar or some tomato wedges.

SERVES 1 *CHAINAK* (PERSON)

Teapot Soup

SHERWA BIRINJ
Rice Soup

This is an economical and simple soup, for which the recipe is flexible. The lamb or chicken may be leftovers, and Afghans might use meatballs instead of meat. The amount of vegetables can be adjusted as you please.

½ cup short-grain rice
2 - 4 oz lamb or chicken, cut into small pieces
¼ cup vegetable oil
1 tbs powdered dill
1 tomato, chopped
1 medium potato, peeled and cubed
1 medium carrot, scraped and cubed
salt and pepper

Wash the rice and put in a large pan and cover with about 4 cups water. Add the meat, oil, dill, vegetables and salt and pepper. Bring to a boil, cover with a lid, leaving it slightly ajar, then turn down the heat and simmer until the rice is soft and the meat and vegetables cooked, stirring from time to time, for about 40 minutes or so.

SERVES 4

KOFTA SHERWA
Meatball Soup with Dill

This soup is sometimes called *sherwa-e-shibit, shibit* meaning "dill." Add more or less rice depending on how thick you would like the soup to be.

8 oz lamb, minced
1 small onion, finely chopped or minced
½ tsp fresh grated ginger (optional)
salt
¼ - ½ tsp red pepper
¼ cup vegetable oil
1 large onion, finely chopped or sliced
2½ to 5 tbs rice, short- or long-grain
2 leeks, washed and chopped
1 tsp turmeric
2 tbs dill weed

Mix the lamb with the small onion and grated ginger. Add salt to taste and half of the red pepper. Mix and knead well until the mixture is smooth, then form into small balls about ½ inch in diameter.

Heat the vegetable oil in a pan and add the large onion. Fry until golden brown. Add 1¾ cups water and bring to a boil. Drop in the meatballs one at a time and allow to boil for a minute or two. Now add the rice, leeks, turmeric, the remaining red pepper, dill and salt. Add 1¾ cups water and bring back to a boil and then reduce the heat and cook gently until the rice is soft and the meatballs are cooked, about 40 minutes.

Serve with bread or *nan.*

SERVES 4

ESHKANA-E-MIWA
Fruit Soup

Eshkana means "without meat." This soup, which is typical of the Herat region, shows the influence of Persia and Central Asia and their liking for sweet and sour flavors.

8 oz dried apricots
8 oz prunes
½ cup vegetable oil
1 medium onion, finely chopped
2 cloves garlic, peeled and crushed
1 tbs vinegar
1 tbs sugar
salt and black pepper
4 small eggs

Soak the apricots and prunes in enough water to cover them and simmer gently for about 1 hour.

Heat the oil and add the onion and garlic. Fry gently until soft and golden brown. Add the apricots and prunes with their water and add extra water to cover by about 1 inch. Bring to a boil then turn down the heat and simmer for a few minutes. Add the vinegar, sugar and salt and black pepper to taste. Simmer for about an hour. Add more water if the soup has thickened too much.

Fifteen minutes before serving break each egg separately in a cup and carefully add one by one to the soup. The soup can be served on its own or with *nan* or pour on to pieces of *nan* in individual bowls. Sprinkle on more black pepper if desired.

SERVES 4

SHERWA-E-PIAWA
Potato Soup

In Afghanistan this is a poor man's soup and is usually made in winter. *Piawa* means "without meat."

6 tbs vegetable oil
2 medium onions, chopped
3 medium potatoes, peeled and cut into 1 inch cubes
1 tsp turmeric
salt and red pepper

Heat the oil in a pan and fry the onions over a medium to high heat until nearly brown. Add the potatoes. Stir and fry until the potatoes are well coated with the oil. Add 3½ to 4 cups water, the turmeric and salt and red pepper to taste. Simmer until the potatoes are cooked, about 20 to 30 minutes.

Serve with fresh *nan.*

SERVES **4**

SHERWA-E-LAWANG
Yogurt Soup with Tomatoes

I first tasted this recipe at the home of my friend, Mrs. Parwin Ali. It comes from the southeast area of Afghanistan. She has kindly sent me her recipe and I find it easy to make.

2 cloves garlic, peeled and crushed
4 tbs margarine or ghee
3 medium tomatoes, skinned and chopped
16 oz yogurt (*chaka* see p. 40)
2 tbs all-purpose flour
½ tsp turmeric
salt

Fry the garlic in the margarine or ghee until brown. Add the tomatoes and stir and fry until reddish-brown.

Blend the yogurt, 1 cup water, the flour, turmeric and salt, either by hand or in a mixer. Then slowly add to the garlic and tomatoes. Bring to a boil, turn down the heat and simmer gently until the soup is thickened, about 30 minutes.

SERVES 3 TO 4

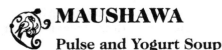

MAUSHAWA
Pulse and Yogurt Soup

In Afghanistan this soup is served either as a starter or as a main meal. This is the original version of *maushawa*, cooked with meat *qorma* but another popular version is made using meatballs *(kofta)*. The meatballs are prepared as for the *kofta* in *kofta chalau* (see p. 158), but are smaller (about ½ inch in diameter). The sauce remains the same too, except that this recipe adds in yogurt. Afghans like to serve this soup "hot," but seasoning can be adjusted according to taste.

2 oz chickpeas
2 oz red kidney beans
2 oz mung beans (or green split peas)
5 tbs short-grain rice
16 oz yogurt (*chaka*, see p. 40)
2 tsp powdered dill
salt

FOR THE MEAT STEW:
3 tbs vegetable oil
1 medium onion, finely chopped
8 oz beef, veal or lamb, cut in ½ inch cubes
1 medium tomato, skinned and chopped
salt
¼ - 1 tsp red pepper

Soak the chickpeas and red kidney beans in water overnight. Put the chickpeas, red kidney beans, mung beans and rice in a large pan with 4 cups water, including the water in which the pulses have been soaked. Bring to a boil, cover leaving the lid slightly ajar, turn the heat to low and simmer. Cook until the pulses are soft (the time this takes depends on the freshness of the pulses).

Meanwhile cook the meat and sauce. Heat the vegetable oil in a pan and add the chopped onion. Fry over a medium heat until soft and reddish-brown. Add the meat and fry again until brown. Add the tomatoes, stirring well and boil for a minute or so. Add ½ cup water, salt and red pepper to taste. Stir well and bring back to the boil. Turn down the heat and simmer until the meat is tender and the sauce thickened.

When cooked, mix all the ingredients; the rice, chickpeas, red kidney beans, together with the juices in which they have cooked, the meat stew, the yogurt, powdered dill and salt to taste. Stir well and add extra water if you want to thin the soup. Continue stirring and simmer for another 5 to 10 minutes to allow the flavors to blend.

Serve the *maushawa* hot in individual soup plates or cups. *Nan* is usually served with this soup.

SERVES 4 TO 6

Street
Foods
and
Snacks

S treet food is very popular in Afghanistan and a variety of tasty snacks can be purchased from street vendors either to eat there or to be taken home. The name for a street vendor is *tabang wala*. A *tabang* is a large flat round wooden tray on which the *tabang wala* carries his wares and stakes his claim to a particular street corner or patch by setting his *tabang* down. Business is often brisk. He provides an assortment of food, catering for the varied tastes and requirements of his customers. The type of food he sells will also depend on the region of Afghanistan and the time of the year. With his smiling, cheerful face, the *tabang wala* will call out to the hungry, tired passersby to come and try his delicious *shour nakhod*, his sweet *sambosa-e-shireen* or to quench their thirst with a glass of his refreshing and sweet *kishmish ab*.

In the winter or early spring, a steaming plate of *pilau-e-tolaki* is very welcome. *Tolaki* means weighed. The *tabang wala* weighs out the *pilau* on scales with various sizes of stones representing ¼ or ½ pound. Boiled, sliced potatoes served with vinegar are also popular, as are boiled eggs. *Pakaura* is another example of a popular street food and can be made from a variety of ingredients; they are usually served with some sort of spicy chutney.

Street vendors are particularly active on festive days such as New Year or *Eid*. Children buy various kinds of sweets, toffees, nuts, roasted chickpeas and so on from the sweet seller in cone-shaped paper bags. They might choose *Khasta-e-shireen*, a kind of nut brittle made by pouring caramel over almonds or apricot kernels. These are made in large round plate-like shapes and children break off pieces to munch on. Crystallized sugar called *nabot* is also very popular.

More permanent food stalls in the bazaar sell *faluda* and ice cream (*sheer yakh*), both very popular in the summer time. *Haleem*, a kind of cereal porridge, is a nourishing winter dish also bought from street stalls. Winter is the time for fish in Afghanistan, so in the winter months there are many food stalls selling what can be described as the Afghan version of fish and chips. The fish is bought fried and served with *jelabi*.

Kishmish panir (cheese with raisins) is a springtime speciality, and corn on the cob is roasted over charcoal and sold to passersby.

Snacks made at home include the crisp, tasty pastries called *boulanee* and *sambosa*.

PAKAURA
Vegetable Fritters

Pakaura are a popular street food in Afghanistan, but they can also be served as tasty snacks or appetizers for a cocktail party. This recipe is for potato *pakaura* but it can also be made with other vegetables such as cauliflower, sliced onions, and eggplant, sliced into thin rounds. The potatoes should be parboiled first.

6 oz (1¼ cups) chickpea flour (besan)
1 tbs salt
½ tsp turmeric
1 tsp ground cilantro seed
    (or 1 tbs finely chopped fresh cilantro)
½ - 1 tsp red pepper
4 medium to large potatoes
vegetable oil for deep frying

Make a batter with the flour and ¾ to 1 cup water and add the salt. Beat well and set aside for half an hour or so. Add the turmeric, cilantro and red pepper.

Meanwhile scrub the potatoes and boil in their skins for 10 to 12 minutes. Leave to cool, then remove the skins and slice thinly into rounds a little less than ¼ inch thick.

Heat the vegetable oil until hot, then dip the potato slices into the batter, coating on both sides. Put into the hot oil and deep fry them several at a time. They will rise to the surface. When golden brown, remove them from the oil and drain on paper towels.

Sprinkle with extra salt and pepper according to taste and serve with a mint, cilantro or red pepper chutney.

SERVES **4**

BOULANEE
Leek-filled Pastries

These are a great favorite among foreigners in Afghanistan and are delicious especially when served with drinks. They should be served crisp and hot, straight from the frying pan. However, Afghans occasionally serve them cold, especially if there are a lot of other dishes being served at the same time. They are made on special occasions such as birthdays and engagements, but can also be served as snacks.

Two types of *boulanee* are prepared in Afghanistan. The most popular is that made with *gandana* (see p. 34) but leeks make a good substitute. *Boulanee* are also made with a mashed potato filling. (See the next recipe). Often at parties or special occasions both types of *boulanee* are prepared at the same time.

    1 lb (3½ cups) sifted all-purpose flour
    3 tsp salt
    1 lb *gandana* or leeks (trimmed weight),
        washed and finely chopped
    ½ tsp red pepper
    1 tbs vegetable oil, plus extra for frying

Put the flour and 1 teaspoon of salt into a mixing bowl. Add slowly as much water as required (about 1 cup) and mix to form a stiff dough. Place the dough onto a clean work surface and knead for 5 to 10 minutes until the dough is elastic, smooth and shiny. Form the dough into a ball, cover with a damp cloth and set aside for at least half an hour.

Squeeze out as much water as possible from the leeks and put into a colander. Add 1 to 2 teaspoons salt and the red pepper. Mix and knead by hand until the leeks begin to soften and then add 1 tablespoon of oil. Mix again before setting aside.

Divide the dough into three or four balls. Roll out each ball as thin as possible on a lightly floured surface (the thickness should be no more than 1/16 inch—if the dough is too thick the *boulanee* will be tough). Take a round cutter of 5 to 6 inches, (a pan lid or tin lid can be used) and cut out as many rounds as possible. The number of *boulanee* will depend on how thinly the dough is rolled out and the size of cutter used. On half of each round spread 2 to 3 tablespoons of the drained leeks. Moisten the edges of the dough, fold over and seal shut. The *boulanee* should be spread out on a lightly floured surface until ready to fry. Do not place one *boulanee* on top of another as they will stick together.

When all the *boulanee* are made and you are ready to serve them, heat enough vegetable oil in a frying pan and shallow fry one or two *boulanee* at a time, browning on both sides. Keep warm until all are finished. Serve at once.

MAKES APPROXIMATELY **15**

A typical Afghan sieve used to produce finer wholemeal flour needed in the preparation of Boulanee.

BOULANEE KATCHALU
Boulanee with a Potato Filling

1 lb (3½ cups) sifted all-purpose flour
3 tsp salt
2 lbs (6 medium) potatoes
2 oz (about 6) scallions, finely chopped
1 tsp black pepper
vegetable oil for frying

Make the dough as for the *boulanee* filled with leeks (p. 70).

Peel and wash the potatoes and boil them in salted water until soft. Drain off the water and mash thoroughly. Add the spring onions, salt and black pepper.

Roll out the dough as for the *boulanee* with leeks and cut out as many rounds as possible. On half of each round spread 1 to 2 tablespoons of the mashed potatoes. Moisten the edges of the dough, fold over and seal shut.

Continue as for the *boulanee* with leeks.

MAKES APPROXIMATELY 15

SAMBOSA GOSHTI
Fried Pastries Filled with Minced Meat

Sambosa are another popular snack and ideal for serving with drinks. They are similar to the Indian *samosa* but are not so hot and spicy. Some Afghans use the same pastry as for *ashak*. Ready-made filo pastry can be used.

1 lb (3½ cups) all-purpose flour
salt

FOR THE FILLING:
1 lb minced meat
4 oz (1 medium) onion, finely chopped
8 tbs vegetable oil or more
1 - 2 tbs garden peas (optional)
1 tsp ground cumin
1 tsp ground cilantro
1 tsp black pepper
1 - 2 hot green chilies, deseeded and finely chopped (optional)
lemon juice
salt
vegetable oil for frying

Sift the flour into a bowl with about ½ teaspoon salt. Add slowly as much water as required (about 1 cup), mixing to form a stiff dough.

Knead for a few minutes until smooth. Form into seven equal balls. Cover with a damp cloth and leave for 15 to 30 minutes.

To prepare the filling, put the meat and chopped onion in a pan with 2 tablespoons of vegetable oil and fry gently for about 15 minutes. Add the peas (if used) and continue frying gently for a further 15 minutes or so. Add the cumin, cilantro, black pepper, chilies, a sprinkling of lemon juice and salt. Cook for a few more minutes, stirring well. Drain off the excess oil and juices.

Roll out each ball of dough into paper thinness on a lightly floured board. Brush six layers with about 1 tablespoon of oil each. Place the layers on top of each other, ending with the seventh layer. Roll out again thinly, trying not to stretch the pastry too much. Cut into 4-inch squares. The number of *sambosa* will vary according to how thinly the dough is rolled out.

Inside each square, spoon about 1 tablespoon of the cooked meat. Fold the filled pastry into a triangle and seal tightly shut. Repeat until all the squares are filled.

Heat enough vegetable oil in a pan to deep-fry the *sambosa* until golden brown on both sides. Remove from the oil and drain.

Sambosa can be served hot or cold, but I think they are tastier hot.

MAKES APPROXIMATELY 24

SHOUR NAKHOD
Chickpeas with a Mint Sauce

Shour means "salty" and this tasty snack is one of the wares sold by street vendors in the bazaars of towns and cities. The cooked chickpeas are mounded on a large platter. The customer will be served with a portion of chickpeas on a small plate or in a small bowl. The mint dressing will then be generously sprinkled over them. A similar dish is made with red kidney beans.

FOR THE CHICKPEAS:
8 oz chickpeas
½ tsp baking soda
1 tsp salt

FOR THE DRESSING:
4 tbs white wine vinegar
½ tsp salt
1 large sprig of mint, finely chopped
2 pinches cayenne pepper

Soak the chickpeas in the 5 cups water for several hours or overnight. Put the chickpeas, with their soaking liquid, in a bowl and add the baking soda. Bring to a boil, skimming off any froth which may form. Boil for 10 minutes, then reduce the heat, cover the pan and simmer slowly on a low heat until the chickpeas are soft but still retain their shape and the liquid has reduced, just leaving a thickened juice in the bottom of the pan. The length of time this takes varies; it can take 3 to 4 hours or more. The secret of this dish really lies in cooking the chickpeas very slowly, stirring from time to time to keep them moist.

Carefully stir in the salt. Leave the chickpeas to cool in their juices. When cooled stir carefully to coat all the chickpeas with the thickened juice.

Meanwhile, mix all the dressing ingredients together with 2 tbs water. Then sprinkle the dressing liberally over the chickpeas, mix it in gently, and sprinkle with more salt, according to taste.

SERVES 4

KISHMISH PANIR
Cheese with Raisins

In the spring it was a common sight in the bazaars of towns and cities to see balls of white cheese, known as *panir-e-khom*, being displayed on a bed of green vine leaves. The cheese, which was brought to market in the towns by people from the mountains or outlying districts, was always sold with red raisins (*kishmish surkh*) to be eaten as an accompaniment.

3½ cups milk
4 tsp fresh lemon juice
a handful of red raisins

Bring the milk to a boil, then remove from the heat and add the lemon juice. The milk will begin to separate. Give a stir and then leave to stand for a while. It will separate into curds and whey. Place in a muslin cloth and stand over a deep bowl to catch the whey. Leave for about 1 to 1½ hours until the whey has dripped through, then gather up the muslin cloth round the curds and tie firmly to form the curds into a roundish cheese. Leave it hanging over the bowl for several hours in a cool place.

When ready to serve the cheese, remove the cloth and cut the cheese into wedges. Serve with the raisins and perhaps some *nan*. This cheese should be stored in a refrigerator and will keep for approximately 4 days.

If salt is added (which helps to preserve the cheese for longer) at the stage just before it is firmly tied up, the cheese is known as *panir-e-shour*.

SERVES 3 TO 4

HALEEM
Cereal and Meat Porridge

Haleem is an ancient dish with seems to have originated in the region of Iran and Afghanistan but has spread to other countries of the Middle East and to India. It is also known by the name *harissa* (meaning "well cooked") in certain Arab countries, but should not be confused with the hot sauce of North Africa also called *harissa*.

It is a kind of porridge usually made with wheat and lamb, but in the past, and to some extent nowadays, with barley. Chicken is sometimes used instead of lamb. Each country has its own variations, especially with regard to accompaniments. For example in India the porridge is cooked with the addition of various "hot" spices.

It is usually bought from special *haleem* shops. Traditionally it is bought early in the morning as a breakfast dish. Men buy *haleem* on Friday mornings after they had been to the *hamam* (public baths) and bring the *haleem* home to their families to eat for breakfast.

Old recipes call for *dumba*, the fat from the tail of the fat-tailed sheep, to use in the cooking, but ghee or vegetable oil can be substituted. This particular recipe includes both lamb and chicken but just one meat may be used, according to preference.

8 oz whole wheat grain
4 oz chicken on the bone
4 oz boneless lamb
1 tbs vegetable oil or ghee
salt and pepper
¼ cup whole milk
2 oz *qymaq* or clotted cream
4 tbs melted butter or ghee
1 tsp cinnamon
1 tsp ground cardamom
superfine sugar

Soak the wheat grains in water overnight. Bring 3½ cups water to a boil, strain the wheat and add to the boiling water. The water should cover the wheat by about 2 inches. Bring to a boil, cover with a lid, reduce the heat and continue boiling gently until the wheat is soft and the water virtually reduced. This can take about 3 hours.

Meanwhile, in another pan add the chicken, lamb and oil. Add just enough water to cover the meat. Season with salt and pepper. Boil gently until the meat is well cooked and a thick juice has formed. Remove from the heat and allow to cool a little. Now discard the bones from the chicken.

When the wheat is soft and cooked, add the chicken and lamb to the wheat with the remaining meat juices. Adjust the seasoning, according to taste. Bring back to a boil again and cook gently until most of the liquid has been absorbed. This may take a couple of hours.

Place the *haleem* in a food processor and blend until a smooth paste is formed. In Afghanistan, pounding the *haleem* is a laborious process to get it to the right consistency and preparations start in the night so as to have the *haleem* ready for their first customers at breakfast time.

Return the *haleem* to the pan, add the milk and heat again. Add the *qymaq* and mix thoroughly.

Either serve on a large dish making a well in the middle and add the melted butter and sprinkle with the cinnamon, cardamom and sugar, or serve in small separate bowls, sprinkle according to taste.

SERVES 4

BURTA
Eggplant Puree

This dip is delicious with fresh warm *nan*. It also goes well with kebabs and *pakaura*.

2 medium eggplants
1 vegetable stock cube
4 cloves garlic, peeled and crushed
1 - 2 hot green chilies, seeded and finely chopped
10 oz yogurt (*chaka*, see p. 40)
salt

Peel the eggplants and cut into slices about ½ inch thick. Place in a pan, add the stock cube and about 1 cup water. Bring to a boil, then reduce the heat and boil gently until tender, 10 to 15 minutes. Leave to cool a little, then remove the eggplants from the liquid with a slotted spoon and place in a blender with about half of the cooking juices. Add the garlic, chilies and 1 tablespoonful of the yogurt. Blend the ingredients together. Finally stir in the rest of the yogurt and add salt to taste.

SERVES 6 TO 10

Pasta
and
Noodle
Dishes

Pasta and noodle dishes are popular in Afghanistan, especially in the north. They play an important part in the diet. Pasta and noodle dishes have a long history and there are many theories about their origins. I subscribe to the view that the product evolved independently in more than one part of the world, especially the Orient and Italy. What is certain is that Afghan pasta dishes are very similar to those of neighboring countries in Central Asia and China. *Mantu*, a steamed pasta, is closely related to the Chinese bread, *man t'ou*, and the *manti* of Turkey. One could also say that some of the Afghan pastas are like some Italian forms: for example, *ashak*, a stuffed pasta, resembles ravioli to some extent and *lakhchak* is similar to lasagne.

To make Afghan pasta can take time, so many Afghans now living in the West substitute the wonton wrappers which are available in Oriental and many regular supermarkets.

AUSH-E-ASLI
Pasta, Yogurt and Meatballs

Aush is a popular dish. It is very versatile and families have their own variations. Afghans often prepare it to cure colds and then they add plenty of garlic and lots of red pepper as they say it helps clear the head and chest. It is filling and is usually eaten as a main course, but smaller quantities can be served as a first course. This recipe is for the original *aush*, known as *aush-e-asli*.

Afghans usually make their own spaghetti or noodles from the same dough used for *boulanee* (p. 70). The dough is rolled out very thinly to 1/16 inch, then rolled up tightly and cut into fine strips with a sharp knife. The spaghetti is then tossed in a little flour and allowed to dry on a board. The spaghetti can be cooked straight away or stored in a covered jar for a couple of days. I have used fresh spaghetti, noodles or tagliatelle in this recipe as it saves time and fresh pasta is now available at many delicatessens and supermarkets.

FOR THE MEATBALLS:
1 lb minced beef or lamb
1 medium onion, minced or grated
1 tsp ground cilantro
1 tsp ground cumin
½ tsp ground black pepper
1 egg (optional)
salt

FOR THE SAUCE:
6 tbs vegetable oil
2 medium onions, minced or grated
1 medium to large tomato, peeled and chopped
salt and pepper

FOR THE *AUSH*:
salt
8 oz fresh spaghetti or tagliatelle
16 oz yogurt (*chaka*, see p. 40)
¼ - ½ tsp red pepper
1 tbs dried mint
2 - 3 cloves garlic, peeled and crushed
oil

First prepare the meatballs. Combine the minced meat, onion, spices, egg and salt and mix thoroughly. Knead until smooth and form into small balls about ½ inch in diameter.

Now prepare the sauce. Heat the vegetable oil in a pan and add the onions. Fry, stirring continuously over a medium to high heat until soft and reddish-brown. Add the tomatoes and stir and fry briskly until the sauce turns brownish. Add 6 tablespoons water, salt and pepper and bring back to simmering point. Add the meatballs, one at a time, in a single layer, then cover, leaving the lid slightly ajar, turn down the heat to low and simmer gently for about half an hour, or until the meatballs and sauce have a browned look and the sauce has thickened. If the sauce is too thick you can add a little water.

To cook the *aush,* put about 3½ cups water into a large pan and bring to a boil. Add plenty of salt and the spaghetti; bring back to a boil, then turn down the heat to medium and cook uncovered and gently for 10 to 15 minutes. Do not drain. Then add the meatballs and sauce, the strained yogurt, red pepper and the mint. Mix and stir well. Turn down the heat to low and leave to simmer slowly for about 10 minutes to let the flavors blend.

Meanwhile, fry the crushed garlic in a little oil and add to the *aush*, then serve hot. Some Afghans like it very thick, others prefer a thinner soup and add extra water.

This dish can be prepared in advance and reheated.

SERVES **4**

AUSH
Pasta with Yogurt, Chickpeas, Kidney Beans and Minced Meat

This is another version of *aush* that is also delicious. The recipe includes chickpeas and red kidney beans and, instead of the meatballs, minced meat *(qima)* is served separately and added on top of the *aush*.

2 oz chickpeas
2 oz red kidney beans
8 oz (225 g) fresh spaghetti or tagliatelle
16 oz yogurt (*chaka*, see p. 40)
1 tbs dried mint
red pepper
salt

FOR THE MINCED MEAT:
6 tbs vegetable oil
2 medium onions, finely chopped
1 lb minced beef or lamb
½ cup tomato juice (or water)
1 tsp ground cilantro
salt and pepper

Soak the chickpeas and beans in 4 cups water overnight.

Put the chickpeas and beans into a large pan with the water in which they were soaked and add ½ cup water. Bring to a boil, then reduce the heat and boil gently until cooked, adding extra water if necessary. Cooking time will vary according to the freshness of the pulses.

While the pulses are cooking, prepare the meat. Heat the oil in a pan over a medium to high heat. Add the chopped onions and fry, stirring continuously until they are reddish-brown. Add the meat and stir well. Fry until brown. Add the tomato juice (or water) and bring to a boil. Add the cilantro, salt and pepper to taste. Stir again, then turn down the heat and simmer for about half an hour or until the meat is cooked. Add extra water if the mixture becomes too dry.

When the meat and pulses are cooked, bring 3½ cups water to a boil in a large pan. Add salt and the spaghetti, and boil gently for 10 to 15 minutes. Add the chickpeas, beans, yogurt, and some or all of the juices from the peas and beans, depending on how thick you want the soup. Add the dried mint, salt and red pepper and mix well. More water can be added if required. Leave on a low heat for about 10 minutes or so to let the flavors blend. Serve the soup and top with a little of the meat. The remaining meat is served separately to be added to the top of each individual portion of *aush*.

This dish can be prepared in advance and reheated.

SERVES 4

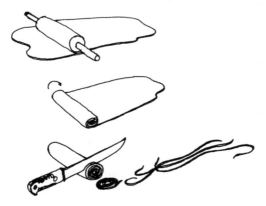

ASHAK
Leek-filled Pasta with Meat Sauce

This delicious and famous pasta dish requires time and patience but the effort is well worth it. Many Afghans, however, for quickness, now substitute wonton wrappers in making this dish. In Afghanistan, the filling is *gandana* (p. 34) but leeks make a good substitute. It is usually served with minced meat *(qima)* and reconstituted *quroot* or *chaka* (strained yogurt).

> 1 lb (3½ cups) all-purpose flour
> 4 tsp salt
> 1 egg
> 2 tbs vegetable oil
> 1 lb washed, finely chopped *gandana* or leeks
>   (trimmed weight)
> ½ tsp red pepper
> 16 oz yogurt (*chaka*, see p. 40)
> 3 cloves garlic, peeled and crushed
> 1 tsp vinegar
> 1 tbs ground mint
>
> FOR THE MEAT SAUCE:
> 6 tbs vegetable oil
> 1 - 2 medium onions, finely chopped
> 1 lb minced beef or lamb
> ½ cup tomato juice or water
> salt and black pepper

Prepare the dough. Sift the flour and 1 teaspoon of salt into a large mixing bowl, make a well and add the egg and 1 tablespoon of oil. Add ½ cup water slowly and knead thoroughly to form a smooth dough. Divide the dough into two balls and cover with a damp cloth for about an hour.

To prepare the meat sauce: Heat the oil in a pan, add the onions and fry, stirring continuously, until they are reddish-brown. Add the meat, stir and fry until brown. Mix in the tomato juice and bring to a boil. Add salt and black pepper to taste. Stir well, then lower the heat and simmer until the sauce is thick and oily (½ to 1 hour). Afghans like it oily but some of the oil can be spooned off.

Squeeze the *gandana* or leeks hard to drain, and place in a colander. Add 1 teaspoon of salt and the red pepper. Knead until the leeks begin to soften and then mix in the other tablespoon of oil.

Roll out one ball of the dough on to a lightly floured surface to a thickness of ¹⁄₁₆ inch (no thicker, or the *ashak* will be tough). Cut out rounds (2½-inch diameter) with a cutter. Put 1 to 2 teaspoons of the drained leeks on half of the rounds. Use the other half to cover the leeks and seal the edges carefully. Place the prepared *ashak* on to a well floured sheet or tray. Do not place on top of each other as they will stick together. Repeat with the remaining dough.

Place the yogurt in a bowl and mix in the garlic and 1 teaspoon of salt. Put half of the yogurt on a flat dish in a warm place.

Bring 7 cups water to a boil in a large pan and add the vinegar and 1 teaspoon of salt. Drop in the *ashak* and boil gently for about 10 minutes, pushing them down carefully with a slotted spoon as they rise to the surface. When cooked, remove with a large slotted spoon or sieve taking care not to break them. Drain thoroughly and place the *ashak* onto the dish on top of the yogurt. Cover with the remaining yogurt and sprinkle over the mint. Top with a little of the minced meat and serve at once together with a separate bowl of meat.

SERVES 4, OR 8 AS A FIRST COURSE

MANTU
Pasta Filled with Meat and Onion

This is the most traditional of all Uzbek dishes. I spent a very enjoyable day with the Rashidzada family, who kindly showed me how to make *mantu*. It is very tasty but does require some preparation. (To make preparation easier many Afghans in the West substitute wonton wrappers instead of making the pasta.)

Uzbeks usually serve *mantu* as an appetizer and then follow it with a *pilau*, such as *qabili pilau Uzbeki*. You will need a large steamer for this recipe. Some people use minced meat to save time, but it works less well as the meat tends to form a hard lump inside the pasta.

Many Afghans like to serve *mantu* with a carrot *qorma* (p. 180) instead of the tomato sauce.

1 lb (3½ cups) all-purpose flour
2 - 3 tsp salt
1 lb boneless fatty lamb, chopped into very small pieces
3 medium onions, finely chopped
1 green chili pepper, finely chopped (optional)
1 - 2 tsp ground black pepper
1 - 2 tsp ground cumin
1 tbs vegetable oil
1 tbs tomato puree
1 tbs finely chopped fresh cilantro
16 oz yogurt (*chaka*, see p. 40)

Prepare the dough. Sift the flour with about 1 teaspoon salt into a mixing bowl. Add, slowly, as much water as required (about 1 cup) and mix to form a stiff dough. Place the dough on a clean work surface and knead for 5 to 10 minutes or until the dough is elastic and shiny. Form the dough into a ball, cover with a damp cloth and set aside, for about an hour.

Put the chopped lamb, onions, chili, 1 to 2 tsp salt, pepper and cumin in a bowl and mix thoroughly.

Divide the dough into four small balls which will make it easier to roll out. Roll out to a thickness of about ¹⁄₁₆ inch on a lightly floured surface. Cut into 4 inch squares. Into each square put about 1 heaped tablespoon of meat mixture. Take two opposite corners and bring them to join in the center by nipping together firmly between your fingers. Nip together the two remaining corners as shown in the drawing. The *mantu* should not be sealed completely as the steam has to be able to penetrate and cook the filling. The method of sealing them varies but I have found this way to be the simplest. Use fat to grease well the shelves of the steamer. This prevents the *mantu* from sticking. Place them on the shelves leaving a small space between each one. Steam for 30 to 45 minutes over a medium heat.

While the *mantu* are steaming, make the tomato sauce. Heat the oil in a pan, add the tomato puree and bring to a boil. Turn down the heat, stir and simmer until the *mantu* are ready.

Remove the *mantu* carefully from the steam shelves and place on a large, warm dish. Spoon the tomato sauce over the top and sprinkle with the chopped cilantro. Serve the yogurt in a separate bowl.

SERVES 4, OR 8 AS A FIRST COURSE

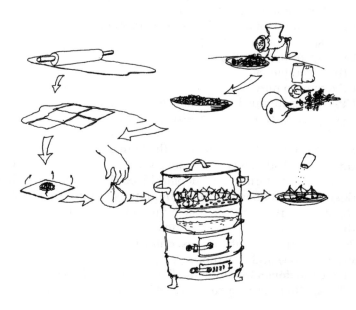

LAKHCHAK
Pasta with Meat Sauce and Yogurt

Lakhchak is a little similar to Italian lasagne. It is simple to make, especially if you buy ready-made fresh lasagne. Alternatively, make the same dough as for *ashak* (p. 84) or for *boulanee* (p. 70).

FOR THE MEAT SAUCE:
6 tbs vegetable oil
2 medium onions, chopped
1 lb minced beef or lamb
½ cup tomato juice or water
1 tsp ground cilantro
salt and pepper

FOR THE *LAKHCHAK*:
2 - 3 cloves of garlic, peeled and crushed
salt
16 oz yogurt (*chaka*, see p. 40)
1 lb fresh *lakhchak* or lasagne
1 - 2 tbs olive oil or corn oil
1 tbs dried mint

Cook the meat as in the recipe for *aush* (p. 81).

Add the peeled and crushed garlic and a little salt to the yogurt.

Cut the *lakhchak* into 2-inch squares, or into any shape you wish. (Do not make the shapes too big or they will be difficult to handle.) If you are making your own homemade dough, roll it out thinly, to about ¹⁄₁₆ inch and cut into shapes.

Boil plenty of salted water in a large pan and add the oil. (This helps prevent the *lakhchak* sticking together.) Add the *lakhchak* one at a time to the boiling water and cook for 10 to 12 minutes. If you cannot cook the *lakhchak* all in one go, cook half and keep them warm while cooking the second batch.

Spoon about one third of the yogurt onto a large, warm dish, then add half of the cooked *lakhchak*. Spoon another third of the yogurt over the top and cover with half of the meat sauce.

Sprinkle with a little of the mint. Add the rest of the *lakhchak*, cover with the remaining yogurt and remaining meat sauce. Sprinkle with the remaining mint. Serve immediately.

SERVES 4 TO 6

VARIATION:
Some Afghans fry chopped *gandana* (p. 34, but you can use leeks) in a little oil and put them between the *lakhchak*; ½ to 1 lb of leeks is enough.

Egg
Dishes

E gg dishes are called either *khagina* or *kuku* in Afghanistan. They are usually described as a sort of omelette, and may be an ancestor of the omelette which evolved in France and has come to be accepted as the standard version in the western world. They are similar to the Spanish tortilla (not to be confused though with the Mexican bread, *tortilla*) and dishes known as *eggah* in the Middle East. They are very versatile and can be served hot or cold. Sweet versions exist and these are often eaten at tea-time.

These dishes make an excellent, quickly made lunch or snack. I remember that *kuku* were very popular with the shopkeepers in Kabul. While out shopping at lunchtime one would often drop into a shop where the shopkeeper would be making a quick, nourishing and tasty snack out of eggs with perhaps some *gandana*, tomatoes or eggplant in a frying pan over a little charcoal brazier. With their characteristic hospitality they would very often invite their customers to join them in their little "feast." At the very least it was customary to accept a little bowl of sweet tea, if offered.

For all the following recipes I used a deep frying pan with a 10-inch diameter. The *kuku/khagina* can be a bit tricky to turn over. I found the easiest way of doing this is to remove the pan from the heat, place a plate on top and carefully turn the frying pan upside down, then slip the *kuku/khagina* back into the pan on the other side. Another method people use is to brown the top of the cooked *kuku* under the grill. Yet another method used, but rarely in Afghanistan, is to bake the *kuku* in the oven at 375°F for 40 to 50 minutes.

KHAGINA-E-GANDANA
Eggs with *Gandana* (or leeks)

My husband's uncle Noor gave me this recipe. It was one of his favorite dishes. Leeks can be substituted for the *gandana* (see p. 34).

6 eggs
8 oz *gandana* or leeks
2 medium tomatoes
1 bunch scallions
1 green chili (optional)
1 tsp baking powder
2 tsp flour
2 tsp salt
black pepper
vegetable oil for frying
1 tbs chopped fresh cilantro

Beat the eggs in a large bowl. Chop up the *gandana*, tomatoes, scallions and chili (with seeds removed) very finely and add to the beaten egg with the baking powder and flour. Mix well and season with salt and pepper.

Heat the vegetable oil in a round, deep frying pan and pour the egg mixture over the hot oil. Reduce the heat to medium, cover with a lid and cook for about 15 minutes until the bottom of the *khagina* is browning and the vegetables are beginning to set in the egg mixture. Now turn the *khagina* over (see p. 92 for the easiest way to do this) and continue cooking over a medium heat for another 10 to 15 minutes. Take care not to overcook the *khagina*, it should remain soft and should not become "leathery."

Garnish with the fresh cilantro and serve with a chutney and fresh bread.

SERVES 4

KUKU-E-TARKARI
Eggs with Vegetables

1 medium potato (floury type)
4 oz spinach
4 oz fresh cilantro
8 scallions, finely chopped
6 eggs
1 - 2 green chilis, seeds removed and finely chopped
1 tsp turmeric
salt and black pepper
vegetable oil for frying

Peel the potatoes and boil in salted water until soft. Then drain and break up the potatoes into small pieces with your hands or very lightly mash them. Set to one side.

Wash the spinach, cilantro and scallions and drain well to remove as much moisture as possible. Chop them all finely.

Beat the eggs in a bowl and add the finely chopped vegetables including the potatoes and green chilies. Season with turmeric and plenty of salt and black pepper. Mix well.

Heat enough oil in a frying pan to cover and pour in the mixture into the hot oil. Reduce the heat to medium, cover with a lid and cook until the *kuku* is browning on the underside and beginning to set. Now turn it over carefully (see p. 92) and cook over a medium/low heat for a further 5 to 10 minutes until firm.

Cut into sections and serve with fresh *nan* and tea. This *kuku* goes particularly well with *chutni murch* (p. 215).

SERVES 4

KUKU-E-BONJON-E-SIA
Eggs with Eggplant

1 medium onion, finely chopped
vegetable oil
2 medium eggplants
salt and pepper
6 eggs
2 tsp flour
1 tsp baking powder

Fry the onions in vegetable oil in a frying pan until soft and golden brown. Peel the eggplants and cut into small pieces or cubes. Add to the onions and continue frying over a medium/high heat until soft and golden brown, adding more oil as necessary. Season well with salt and pepper.

Beat the eggs with the flour and baking powder. Turn up the heat to high and pour the eggs over the vegetables. Turn down the heat to medium, cover with a lid and cook for about 20 minutes until the mixture is almost set and firm. Turn over (see method on p. 92) to cook the other side for a further 10 or 15 minutes.

Season again with salt and pepper and serve hot with fresh *nan* and a salad.

SERVES 4

KHAGINA-E-BONJON-E-RUMI
Eggs with Tomato

6 eggs
2 medium (8 oz) tomatoes, chopped
1 medium onion, finely chopped
1 small bunch of cilantro, washed and finely chopped
1 - 2 green chili peppers, seeded and finely chopped
1 tbs flour
vegetable oil
salt and pepper

Beat the eggs. Mix together the chopped tomatoes, onion, cilantro (reserve a little for garnishing) and chili in a bowl. Stir in the flour and add the beaten eggs. Mix well.

Add enough oil to cover the bottom of a frying pan and heat. When hot pour over the egg mixture, then turn down the heat to medium, cover and cook for 15 to 20 minutes or until the eggs are set. Turn over carefully as described on p. 92 and cook for another 5 to 10 minutes until brown. Season with salt and pepper.

Garnish with the reserved chopped cilantro and serve with *nan* and perhaps a bowl of yogurt.

SERVES 4

 KHAGINA SHIREEN

Sweet Omelette with Potatoes

This *khagina* is sweet, more like a sort of potato cake. A savory version can be made without the syrup, in which case the *khagina* is sprinkled liberally with red pepper. Chopped onions can also be added to the savory version; if used, they should be fried in a little oil before adding the egg and mashed potatoes.

2 medium (8 oz) potatoes (floury type)
vegetable oil
4 eggs
½ cup sugar

Peel the potatoes and boil in salted water until cooked. Drain and then break up the potatoes with your hand into small pieces or very lightly mash them.

Beat the eggs and pour over the lightly mashed potatoes. Heat enough oil to cover the bottom of a frying pan and when hot add the egg and potato mixture. Turn down the heat to medium, cover with a lid and continue cooking for about 10 minutes or so until the mixture is browning on the underside and the egg is set. Turn over carefully (see p. 92) and fry the other side gently over a medium heat until brown.

While the eggs are cooking mix the sugar with ¼ cup water in a small pan and bring to a boil. Boil gently for a couple of minutes until syrupy. Now pour the hot syrup over the egg and potato mixture and allow the syrup to be absorbed. Cut into serving-size portions and serve with *nan* and tea. This *khagina*, like the others, can be served warm or cold.

SERVES **4**

KABABI

TSCHARIKARI

A kebab stall.

Kebabs

In every town and city of Afghanistan there are numerous kebab stalls or restaurants. Often, while walking round the bazaars, I would find myself drawn to them by the sound of the local Afghan or Indian music and the aroma of the kebabs sizzling over the hot charcoal. Kebab stalls (*dukan-e-kebabi*) were quite basic on the whole: some had chairs and tables and sold soft drinks such as Coca Cola or Fanta; other were just a stall and one would eat the tasty, succulent kebabs while standing around the stall or walking along the street. The *kebabi* (stallholder) would be sitting behind his *manqal* (charcoal brazier), wafting his *pakka* (kebab fan) over the coals to keep them glowing and turning the kebabs over from time time, often gossiping or chatting to one of his customers at the same time. Sometimes he would have an assistant, usually a young boy learning the trade, who would fan the charcoal from the front.

Kebabs from kebab stalls are usually made with lamb, the favored meat in Afghanistan, and either cubed, on the bone, or minced. They are cooked by grilling over charcoal on kebab skewers called *sikh*. Other specialities include liver, kidney or testicle kebabs. *Chapati* or *lawausha,* or sometimes *nan*, are served with the kebabs, along with sliced onions and tomatoes or perhaps a salad. For added flavor they are sprinkled with crushed grape seeds and red pepper. For a "take-away," the crushed seeds and pepper are placed in little cone-shaped paper bags, the kebabs being "wrapped up" in the *lawausha* bread.

Some types of kebabs are fried, and some are baked in a *tandoor* or other oven. *Kebab-e-chopan* is a very simple and basic kebab named after the shepherds (*chopan*) who would make this kebab for themselves in the open after they had made a fire in the crisp night air while watching over their flock of sheep. In the embers of the fire they would roast chunks of meat and lamb fat, which they would first have rubbed with plenty of salt, and then skewered on twigs or small branches.

Kebabs are usually followed by plenty of sweet green tea flavored with cardamom, as this helps the digestion.

I have included in this section some recipes for meat dishes which are not really kebabs but resemble them in being served with bread rather than rice. They are *do piaza*, a lamb dish cooked with onions and split peas, and *qorma rui nan*, a meat dish served with fried bread, *chaka* and *gandana* (or leeks). I have also given one fish kebab recipe, which is very good.

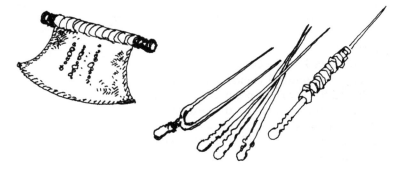

Pakka *and* sikh *for kebabs.*

SIKH KEBAB or TIKKA KEBAB
Lamb Kebab

Of all kebabs these are the most favored by Afghans and are the best known. The kebabs are traditionally cooked over a charcoal fire. Use a barbecue if you have one. Otherwise, an electric oven or gas grill is satisfactory, although of course the flavor will not be the same. The lamb is threaded on kebab skewers *(sikh)*. If using an ordinary grill, balance the skewers on the rim of the grill pan in such a way that all the meat juices drip inside the tray.

Sikh kebabs are always served with bread of some kind, usually *chapati* or *lawausha,* and crushed grape seeds and red pepper are sprinkled on the top for added flavor.

3 tbs lemon juice
4 cloves garlic, peeled and crushed
½ cup live, natural yogurt (optional)
salt and black or red pepper
1 tsp ground cilantro seed (optional)
2 lbs boneless lamb, cut into ¾-inch cubes
8 oz lamb fat (optional) or 2 tbs vegetable oil
2 *lawausha* or *chapati* (or *nan)*

FOR THE GARNISH:
tomato
onion
lemon or lime wedges

Mix the lemon juice, crushed garlic, yogurt (if used), salt, pepper and cilantro in a bowl. Add the lamb and lamb fat (if used) or oil. Mix well and marinate, covered, in the refrigerator for several hours or overnight.

Preheat the grill. Thread the meat on to the skewers. (The cubes of meat should be alternated with the fat, if used.) Grill, turning frequently, for about 15 to 20 minutes until brown and cooked.

Place the *lawausha* or *chapati* on a large dish, remove the kebabs from the skewers and place them on the bread. Sprinkle with a little salt and pepper, garnish with the tomato, onion and lemon, and fold the *chapati* or *lawausha* over to keep the kebabs warm. The extra *lawausha* or *chapati* is cut into pieces and served separately. A mixed salad is a good accompaniment.

SERVES 4

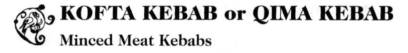 KOFTA KEBAB or QIMA KEBAB
Minced Meat Kebabs

These kebabs sometimes also go by the name *lola* meaning "round," because of their shape. Cooked in the same way as *sikh kebab,* this kebab is made with minced meat.

1 medium to large onion
3 cloves garlic, peeled and crushed
2 lbs best minced beef or lamb
salt and black or red pepper
2 *lawausha* or *chapati*

FOR THE GARNISH:
fresh mint or cilantro
lemon wedges

Mince the onions and mix thoroughly with the garlic and meat, adding salt and pepper. Continue mixing well with the hand until the mixture becomes sticky. Then wet your hand with water and mold the mixture round kebab skewers to form kebabs about 4 inches long and 1 inch in diameter. Press onto the skewers firmly so that they will hold. Smooth the kebabs carefully with your wet hand.

Preheat the grill. Grill the kebabs over a high heat. When they are brown on both sides, reduce the heat to medium and grill, turning frequently, for about 15 minutes more.

Remove carefully from the skewers and serve on one of the breads. Sprinkle with a little salt and black or red pepper. Garnish with fresh mint or cilantro and lemon wedges. Fold the bread over to keep the kebabs warm. The remaining bread, cut into pieces, is served with them.

SERVES **4**

NARGIS KEBAB
Meatballs Stuffed with Egg

Sometimes called *Kofta-e-nargis*, *nargis* means "narcissus" in Persian, the name of this dish was given because of the way the *kofta* is made to resemble a flower.

    8 small eggs
    4 medium onions
    2 lb minced lamb
    4 oz fresh cilantro, washed and finely chopped
    2 egg yolks
    2 egg whites
    salt and pepper
    ½ tsp ground ginger (optional)
    1 tbs flour (optional)
    vegetable oil
    4 tbs tomato puree
    3 tsp ground cilantro

Hard boil eggs; this will take about 7 minutes. Grate or finely chop three of the onions.

Mix the minced lamb, onions, half of the fresh cilantro, 2 egg yolks and 1 egg white, salt and pepper and the ginger, if used. The flour can be used if the mixture is too wet and sticky. Knead the mixture well with your hand until smooth.

Chop the remaining onion and fry gently in oil until golden brown and soft. Add the tomato puree and stir vigorously over a medium to high heat until browning. Add about 3 cups of water, salt, pepper and the ground cilantro. Bring to a boil. Stir well and then reduce the heat and simmer.

Meanwhile, divide the mince mixture into 8 equal portions. Form and knead each portion into a smooth ball, then make a dent and push into it one of the hard-boiled eggs (removing the shell first). Fold the mixture around the egg until there are no gaps and the ball of mince is smooth and round. Dip your fingers into the remaining egg white and smooth around the meatball. (This helps prevent the meatball from breaking or splitting during cooking). Repeat with the remaining eggs and mince.

Add the meatballs carefully to the simmering sauce one at a time and in one layer, shaking the pan gently from time to time. The meatballs should be covered by sauce; if not, add a little more water. Bring back to a boil, then reduce the heat and cook gently until the liquid has reduced and thickened, about 40 to 45 minutes.

To serve, gently remove a meatball, and carefully cut a cross into it. Open carefully, forming into a flower shape. Repeat with the remaining meatballs and into the center of each sprinkle the remaining chopped fresh cilantro. The sauce is served separately. Eat with fresh *nan* or *chalau*.

MAKES 8

SHINWARI KEBAB
Lamb Chops Kebab

Shinwari is the name of one of the large Pashtun tribes of the North West Frontier region. This kebab was one of our favorites and we used to invite our friends to the old town of Kabul, by the river, to go and eat it at one of the kebab stalls there. One was owned by a big man called Pahlwan, which means "wrestler." Other specialities he used to make were *kebab-e-gourda* (kidney kebab) and *kebab-e-kalpura* (lambs' testicles) which was considered a delicacy and an aphrodisiac.

Shinwari kebab is extremely simple to prepare. A similar kebab, often made from ribs of veal, is called *qaburgha* which means "ribs."

12 - 16 best end neck lamb chops, cut thinly
salt and black or red pepper
nan or *chapati*

FOR THE GARNISH:
tomato, sliced or quartered
onion, very finely sliced
lemon wedges

Rub the chops all over, but lightly, with salt. Leave in a cool place for 15 to 30 minutes.

Put the chops onto kebab skewers and either cook over charcoal or under a preheated broiler for about 20 minutes, turning the kebabs frequently, until brown and cooked.

Remove from the skewers, sprinkle with plenty of pepper and serve on fresh *nan* or *chapati*. Garnish with the tomato, onion and lemon.

SERVES 4

KARAYI KEBAB
Lamb Kebab with Eggs

This kebab is prepared individually in round metal pans called *karayi* which are similar to those used for cooking and serving lasagne or cannelloni in restaurants. It can, however, be made quite satisfactorily in a frying pan.

1 - 1½ lbs boneless lamb with fat, cut into ¾-inch cubes
1 - 2 tbs lemon juice
2 cloves garlic, peeled and crushed
½ cup yogurt
vegetable oil for frying
salt and black or red pepper
4 - 8 eggs

Prepare and cook the meat as for *sikh kebab* (p. 102).

When the kebabs are cooked, remove from the skewers and heat the vegetable oil in a large frying pan. Add the kebabs and fry quickly for a few seconds, then break the eggs over the top of the meat and fry until the eggs are cooked. Do not stir the eggs or break them. Sprinkle with salt and pepper and serve straight from the pan, with freshly baked *nan* and a salad.

SERVES 4

VARIATIONS:

Some Afghans fry sliced onions until soft and then add the kebab. This kebab can also be made with meatballs *(kofta)*.

SHAMI KEBAB or LOLA KEBAB
Sausage-shaped Kebabs

I often make these tasty kebabs for buffet parties. They are ideal as they can be prepared in advance and served either cold or warmed up again in the oven. They are particularly good with a chutney and *nan*.

2 lbs boneless lamb, veal or beef, cut into 1-inch cubes
3 medium onions, quartered
2 oz split peas
3 medium (1 lb) potatoes
1 hot green chili pepper, seeds removed, finely chopped
1 sweet red or green bell pepper, finely chopped
2 cloves garlic, peeled and crushed
4 tsp ground cilantro
2 eggs
salt and pepper
vegetable oil for frying

Boil the meat, onions and split peas in 1 cup water until the meat is tender and the split peas soft, about 1 to 1½ hours.

Peel and boil the potatoes separately until soft, then drain well. Mash them and set aside.

Mince the meat, onions, chili pepper, sweet pepper and garlic together. (If using a food processor, do not blend for too long or the mixture will become too "sloppy.") Add the cilantro, eggs, potatoes, salt and pepper and mix well. The mixture should be soft, but firm and not too runny. Add some or all of the remaining stock if it is firm enough, but if it is a little "sloppy" you can add up to ¾ cup flour. With portions of the mixture, form sausage-shaped kebabs, each about 4 inches long and 1 inch in diameter.

Deep-fry the kebabs in hot oil, over a medium to high heat, turning carefully until all sides are golden brown and the kebabs are cooked through.

Serve with fresh *nan* or *chapati* and garnish with fresh mint, cilantro or parsley, tomatoes, scallions and lemon slices or wedges.

MAKES ABOUT **25**

SHAMI KEBAB II
Sausage Kebabs

This is a quick way of making *shami* or *lola* kebab.

    4 medium potatoes
    1½ lbs best minced lamb
    1 large onion, grated or finely chopped
    1 egg
    ½ - 1 tbs flour
    2 tsp ground cilantro seeds
    2 tsp powdered dill weed
    1 tsp turmeric
    salt and red pepper to taste
    vegetable oil for frying

Peel, wash and boil the potatoes until soft and then mash them.

Combine the minced lamb, mashed potatoes, onion and all the other ingredients. Mix thoroughly and knead until the mixture becomes smooth and a bit sticky.

Form into sausage-size shapes and then fry in deep, hot oil. When sealed on all sides, reduce the heat to medium and cook gently until the kebabs are cooked through and golden brown on all sides.

Serve with *nan* and a chutney.

MAKES ABOUT 24

CHAPLI KEBAB
A "Hot" Kebab

Chapli means "sandal" in Dari and this kebab is shaped like the sole of a sandal. It comes from the Jalalabad region and can be very "hot" and fiery. A similar kebab is made in Pakistan. The amount of scallions and chili can be adjusted according to taste.

    1 lb best minced lamb or beef
    1 - 2 large bunches (about 12 oz) scallions, finely chopped
    ¾ cup all-purpose flour
    ½ sweet bell pepper, green or red, finely chopped
    2 - 4 hot green chilies, finely chopped
    3 - 4 tbs, finely chopped fresh cilantro
    2 tsp ground cilantro
    salt
    vegetable oil for frying

Put the meat, scallions, flour, both kinds of pepper, fresh and ground cilantro in a bowl and mix thoroughly, adding salt to taste. Shape the mixture into flat oblongs 6 by 4 inches and ¼ inch thick.

Heat enough vegetable oil in a frying pan to fry the kebabs (which should be almost covered by the oil), and fry over a medium to high heat until they are brown on both sides and cooked through (about 10 minutes).

Serve with a tomato and onion salad and *chapati* or *nan*. Garnish with fresh cilantro and lemon.

MAKES 12

KEBAB-E-DAYGI
Kebab Cooked in a Pan

A recipe given to me by Parwin Ali. She used to cook this kebab for us at her home. It is simple to prepare.

2 lbs lamb on the bone
½ cup live, natural yogurt
2 cloves garlic, peeled and crushed
salt
1 tsp ground cilantro
2 medium (8 oz) onions, finely sliced

Cut the meat into serving-size pieces, and then marinate in the yogurt, garlic, salt and cilantro mixed together. Leave for at least a couple of hours in the refrigerator.

Put the meat and yogurt mixture in a pan and cook gently until the meat is just tender. When it is tender, add the sliced onions and cook further over a medium to low heat until the sauce thickens, the onions have become very soft and the fat from the meat has separated. Stir frequently. Serve with *nan* or *chapati,* or with plain boiled potatoes.

SERVES 4

KEBAB-E-DOSHI
Oven Kebab

Kebab-e-doshi means "oven kebab." However, this kebab is not cooked in the oven, but in a pan on top of the stove. It is easy to make. It contains a lot of onion but the amount can be reduced, if wished. Some Afghan friends, from the Panjshir valley, have told me that they call this kebab *do piaza*.

      10 tbs vegetable oil
      8 medium onions (2 lb) onions, finely sliced
      2 lbs lamb on the bone, cut into serving-sized pieces
      2 tsp ground cilantro
      salt and pepper
      1 green bell pepper, seeded and finely sliced (optional)
      1 green chili (optional)
      7 oz can chopped tomatoes or 1 cup water

Heat the oil in a large pan and add half of the onions. Fry over a medium to high heat until reddish-brown. Add the meat and fry further until the meat is browned, stirring frequently. Add the cilantro, salt and pepper. Cook over a medium heat for 15 minutes, then add the rest of the onions, the green bell pepper (if used), green chili (if used), and the tomatoes. Stir well, cover and cook slowly until the meat is really tender, for about 1 to 1½ hours. There should not be too much liquid. If there is, uncover the pan and cook further to reduce it. Adjust seasoning according to taste.

Serve with fresh *nan* or *chapati*.

SERVES 4

KEBAB-E-MURGH
Chicken Kebab

Chicken is an expensive meat in Afghanistan, so chicken dishes are usually prepared for special occasions, such as an engagement or wedding party. They have a tendency to be dry and even a little tough, so plenty of oil is used. As chickens in the West can be fatty, I have adjusted the amount of oil accordingly.

1 medium chicken
¼ cup vegetable oil
salt and pepper
2 - 3 cloves garlic, peeled and crushed
2 - 3 tbs tomato puree
fresh mint or cilantro and lemon wedges for garnishing

Rub the prepared chicken with 2 tablespoons of the oil, and sprinkle with salt and pepper and the garlic.

Cook in a preheated oven at 350°F or on a rotisserie for 1½ to 2 hours or until browned, cooked through and tender. During the last half hour of cooking, mix the remaining 2 tablespoons of oil and the tomato puree together and spoon over the chicken. Baste frequently.

Serve hot with *nan* or *chapati* and garnish with fresh mint or cilantro and lemon wedges.

SERVES 4

KEBAB-E-MURGH II
Chicken Kebab

This recipe is quite flexible. You can use just chicken legs, or wings, if preferred. The amount of lemon and garlic can also be increased if wished and some Afghans would add a little cilantro seed or chopped chili pepper for that extra "bite."

1 medium chicken
juice of half a lemon, diluted with a little water
2 tbs oil
1 small onion, finely chopped
3 - 4 cloves garlic, peeled and crushed
1 - 2 green chilies, seeds removed, finely chopped (optional)
1 tsp ground cilantro seed (optional)
salt and pepper
fresh mint or cilantro for garnish

Cut the chicken up into serving-size pieces and marinate in the lemon juice, oil, onion, garlic, chilies and cilantro (if used) and salt and pepper. Leave in the refrigerator or a cool place for 4 to 6 hours.

Fry the chicken pieces over a medium heat until brown and cooked through, about 30 to 40 minutes. Serve on *nan* or *chapati,* garnished with fresh mint or cilantro.

Alternatively, preheat the grill, brush the chicken pieces with oil and grill under a medium to high heat for 20 minutes, then turn over, brush with oil again and grill for a further 20 to 30 minutes. Another alternative is to cook the chicken with the marinade in a 425°F oven, for about 30 minutes to 1 hour, turning over to brown all the sides evenly.

SERVES 4

MURGH-E-SHEKAM PUR
Stuffed Chicken

The green pistachios, red raisins, orange peel, yellow split peas and white almonds used as the stuffing in this dish are like jewels tumbling out of a treasure chest. An even more elaborate dish, *pilau-e- murgh-e-shekam pur*, is often made for special occasions in Afghanistan. The whole stuffed chicken is itself cooked inside a *pilau*, see p. 152.

1 oz yellow split peas
peel of 1 orange
2 oz red raisins
2 oz almonds and pistachios, blanched and cut into slivers
1 - 2 tbs vegetable oil
2 oz minced lamb
1 tsp ground green cardamom
salt and pepper
1 medium chicken
6 tbs butter
¼ tsp saffron

Wash the split peas and leave to soak in warm water for about an hour, then boil them in plenty of water until soft.

Peel the orange, removing as much pith as possible and cut into matchstick-size strips. (I find it easier to use a potato peeler to do this.) To remove any bitter taste, put the orange strips into a strainer and dip first in boiling water and then cold. Repeat this a few times, then set aside.

Fry the raisins, almonds and pistachios gently in the oil for a couple of minutes. Remove and set to one side. Now fry the mince in the same oil until brown. Remove and set to one side to cool.

Mix the mince, the raisins, pistachios, almonds and cooked split peas together in a bowl. Add the ground cardamom and salt and pepper to taste.

Stuff the chicken with this mixture. Place the chicken on a sheet of foil large enough to be able to seal and enclose the whole chicken.

Melt the butter in a pan and add the saffron and pour over the chicken. Fold over and seal the foil and place in a preheated oven at 375°F. Cook for about 1 hour, then open up the foil, baste the chicken with the juices and cook further for about half an hour or perhaps a little longer until the chicken is golden brown and tender.

Serve with fried potatoes and lemon wedges and perhaps a salad.

SERVES 4

KEBAB-E-JIGAR
Liver Kebab

Afghans eat all parts of an animal and liver is one of their favorites. This is a very simple and quick recipe for cooking liver.

    2 - 3 tbs oil
    3 - 4 large onions, finely sliced
    1 - 2 tsp ground cilantro seeds
    salt and pepper
    1 lb lambs liver, cut into strips

Heat the oil in a large frying pan and add the sliced onions. Soften and fry until they are just beginning to brown. Add the cilantro, salt and pepper and stir. Now add the liver and fry over a medium heat to seal. Then continue to fry gently for a further 4 to 5 minutes stirring from time to time. Do not overcook the liver or it will become hard and leathery.

Serve with warm fresh *nan* and perhaps with a salad.

SERVES 3 TO 4

🐘 DO PIAZA

Boiled Lamb with Onions, On Bread

Do piaza literally means "two onions." The lamb is boiled with red onions and then served garnished with white onions, sliced and marinated in white vinegar. Afghans traditionally cook this dish with *dumba*, the fat from the tail of the fat-tailed sheep. I find that shoulder of lamb gives this dish a good flavor. It is also served liberally sprinkled with freshly ground black pepper—another matter for individual taste. *Do piaza* is usually served on large *chapati* or *lawausha* but *nan* can be substituted. It is an ideal dish for buffet parties as the meat can be cooked in advance and it can be served hot or cold.

1 large white onion, finely sliced in rings
½ cup white vinegar
2 lbs lamb on the bone, preferably with plenty of fat
2 medium red onions, finely chopped
2 oz split yellow peas
salt and black pepper
chapati, lawausha or *nan*

Marinate the white onion rings in the vinegar for at least 2 hours. (If the vinegar is strong, dilute with water.)

Put the lamb, red onions, and half of the split peas in a pan and cover with about 2 cups water. Season with salt and pepper. Bring to a boil, skimming off the froth from the peas. Turn down the heat and simmer until the meat is tender and the split peas are cooked and soft.

Cook the remaining split peas in plenty of water until soft but not mushy. (I have found that the split peas cooked with the meat often do become mushy. But they do give extra flavor and this dish does benefit from long, slow cooking to bring out the flavor of the meat, so I always cook some split peas separately to make sure I have plenty for garnishing the top of the lamb.)

When you are ready to serve, remove the meat and split peas from the soup with a slotted spoon and place on a *chapati* or *nan*. Add the other split peas on top. Drain the vinegar from the white onions and place them on top of the lamb and split peas. Sprinkle plenty of freshly ground pepper, then cover with another *chapati* or *nan*. (The remaining soup can be kept as stock.)

SERVES 4

DO PIAZA II
Boiled Lamb with *Olu Bokhara* or Prunes

I was interested to read in Abdullah Afghanzada's book, *Local Dishes of Afghanistan,* about an Afghan tradition which I had not heard of before. He relates that when a child is born, a lamb is sacrificed. The lamb is cooked (he does not say how, but perhaps in the same manner as this recipe) and then all the meat is taken from the bones and reserved. The bones are then wrapped in a cloth and buried. This ritual was believed to remove all evil from the newborn child. Mr. Afghanzada then gives a recipe, which I have adapted as follows. As in the previous recipe I find that shoulder of lamb works well for this dish.

> 2 lbs lamb on the bone, preferably with plenty of fat
> vegetable oil
> 2 medium red onions, finely chopped
> salt
> 2 oz split peas, soaked
> 8 *olu bokhara* or prunes
> ¼ tsp saffron or turmeric
> black pepper
> *chapati, lawausha* or *nan*
> 1 medium white onion, finely sliced in rings
> 1 tsp dried mint or 1 tbs finely chopped fresh mint
> 1 lemon or Seville orange

Cut the meat into serving-size portions and rub with oil. Place in a pan and add just enough water to cover the lamb by about

¾ inch. Bring to a boil and remove any scum that forms. Add the chopped red onions and salt and cook gently until the meat is tender, about 1 to 1½ hours.

Meanwhile bring the split peas to a boil in plenty of water, then simmer until tender.

When the meat is cooked remove from the pan and remove all the meat from the bones. Place the boneless meat back in the pan with the broth and add the cooked split peas and the *olu bokhara*. Continue cooking gently until the liquid has reduced, and then add the saffron. Season with salt and pepper.

When ready to serve, remove the meat and split peas from the broth and place the meat on top of the *chapati, lawausha* or *nan*, add the sliced onions on top and sprinkle with mint and decorate with sliced lemon or Seville orange (*norinj*).

SERVES 4

QORMA-E-RUI NAN
Meat Stew with Leeks and Bread

This tasty dish is a good way to use up leftover *nan*. Beef can be used instead of lamb. In Afghanistan *gandana* (see p. 34) are used, but leeks are a good substitute.

½ cup vegetable oil
1 large onion, chopped
1 lb boneless lamb, cut into ½-inch cubes, or minced lamb
½ cup tomato juice or water
salt
½ tsp black pepper
1 lb leeks or *gandana*
2 *nan*
16 oz yogurt or *chaka* (see p. 40)
¼ - ½ tsp red pepper
1 tbs dried mint

Heat ¼ cup of the vegetable oil in a pan over a medium to high heat. Fry the chopped onion, stirring continuously until reddish-brown. Add the meat, stir well and fry until brown. Add the tomato juice and bring to a boil, season with salt and black pepper, stir well, then turn down the heat to low and simmer until the meat is cooked. If necessary add more water. The sauce should be thick and any excess oil can be spooned off.

While the meat is cooking, wash and chop the leeks finely, and drain them well.

When the meat is cooked, cut the *nan* into 4-inch triangles or squares and fry in the remaining ¼ cup oil until lightly browned but not too crisp. Keep warm. Fry the leeks over a medium heat in the same oil until soft, adding a little extra oil if necessary and perhaps a little water to help soften; season with a little salt and pepper to taste.

To serve, cover the bottom of a large, warmed dish with about half of the yogurt, then cover with most of the fried *nan*. Top with the leeks, add the remaining yogurt, and lastly add the meat. Sprinkle with the red pepper and the mint and garnish with the remaining *nan*. Serve hot.

SERVES 4 TO 6

KEBAB-E-DAYGI-E-MAHI
Fish Kebab

To be as authentic as possible it is best to use trout for this kebab. However, I have also used fillets of cod very successfully. *Ghooray angoor* is a flavoring made with small young sour green grapes which are dried in the sun, then ground. It gives a tart or slightly sour flavor to a dish. It can be purchased from Persian shops, but lemon juice can be substituted.

4 trout
1 large onion, shredded
1 carrot, roughly chopped
lemon juice
salt
6 tbs vegetable oil
4 cloves garlic, crushed
1 tsp ground cilantro seed
2 tbs finely chopped fresh cilantro
1 tsp *ghooray angoor* or 1 tsp lemon juice
black or red pepper
fresh mint and lemon wedges

Poach the fish for about 10 minutes in a shallow pan of water, to which has been added a little of the shredded onion (reserve the rest), carrot and a little lemon juice and salt. When cooked remove the trout from the liquid and allow to cool. Remove the skin and take the flesh off the bones and flake.

Gently fry the remaining shredded onions and crushed garlic in 3 tablespoons of the oil, then add the flaked fish. Now add the ground cilantro, the fresh cilantro, *ghooray angoor* and black or red pepper and mix well. Brush the bottom of a casserole with the remaining 3 tablespoons oil and add the chopped up fish mixture. Cover with a lid or foil and bake in a preheated oven at 350°F for about half an hour.

Garnish with sprigs of mint and lemon slices. Serve with fresh *nan*. It is also good with boiled or fried potatoes.

SERVES 4

VARIATION:
An alternative to this recipe is to mash or finely chop up the fish mixture, adding a little flour to help it bind, and form into balls. Fry in shallow oil.

Main Dishes

RICE

A ll the recipes in this chapter are either rice dishes or dishes
served with rice. Afghans love rice, and their many rice
dishes, especially the *pilau* ones, are renowned for their
delicious flavors. Two types of rice are used: long-grain and short-
grain. The long-grain is used for *pilau* and *chalau*, the short-grain
for *bata, shola* and rice desserts.

Chalau is a basic dish of white long-grain rice. It is cooked very
simply with water, a little oil, salt, and sometimes added spices, the
most common one being cumin. *Chalau* is usually accompanied by
a vegetable or a meat dish such as one of the many *qormas*.

Pilau, in contrast, is cooked with meat and meat juices, and
the rice is always colored by one method or another. The most
common agents for coloring *pilau* are browned onions or
caramelized sugar, but saffron and turmeric are also used. A *pilau*
normally has some sort of meat buried in the center of the rice. If
using chicken for their *pilau*, Afghans usually cook and serve it
whole under the rice. (If you do this, you must choose a pan or
casserole large enough to take the whole chicken with the rice,
and you may have a problem when it comes to serving portions
to guests.)

Afghans, by the way, cook huge quantities of rice, with rela-
tively little meat, and use more oil in cooking rice than people in
the West. In my recipes I have already adjusted quantities to
allow for this, but they can of course be further adjusted.

Pots for cooking rice.

COOKING LONG-GRAIN RICE

Afghans use two methods for cooking long-grain rice.

Dampokht method. The rice is boiled in just enough liquid (water or stock) for the cooking. Oil and spices are added to the water at the beginning of the cooking. The rice is finished off in the oven or on top of the stove.

Sof method. The rice is parboiled in a large amount of salted water, then the water is drained off. Oil, more liquid (water or stock) and spices are added at this stage, before the cooking is completed, and the rice is then finished off in the oven or on top of the stove.

Not many Afghans have ovens, especially in the provinces, and the traditional way of cooking rice is in a large *dayg* (cooking pot) over wood or charcoal. Hot coals are placed on top of the lid of the pot to ensure an even heat to dry off the rice.

However, many Afghans nowadays finish off their rice on top of the cooker. They often place a thick, clean cloth over the pan or pot before putting on the lid. The cloth absorbs extra moisture and is also a help if the lid does not fit tightly. They also make several holes in the rice with their *kafgeer* before covering the pan; these holes allow steam to escape.

Which method—*dampokht* or *sof*—is used for cooking *chalau* or *pilau* depends very much on the individual; choose the one you find simplest and which gives the best results for you. My Afghan family tended to use the *dampokht* method, but many Afghans prefer the *sof* method as it is less likely to leave the rice sticky.

There is something to be added about the *sof* method. Many Afghans, when they add the meat juices, or water, with the spices and oil, boil the rice again for a couple of minutes over a high heat with the lid on, until the rice catches on the bottom of the pan and a ticking noise is heard. This results in a crust of rice being formed at the bottom of the pan. This crispy rice is called *tie daygi*. After the rice has been served, the *tie daygi* is scraped off the bottom of the pan and served on a separate plate. It is considered a delicacy. However, this method can easily result in burned rice and a ruined pan! You must stay by the pan and listen carefully for the ticking noise.

A little *tie daygi* is usually formed anyway, and this applies to rice cooked by the *dampokht* method, too. What I have just explained is how to obtain much more than the usual small amount.

Here are a few general tips for cooking long-grain rice.

- Always use a heavy pot or pan with a tightly fitting lid, preferably one which can be put in the oven. I have found my cast-iron casserole invaluable for cooking rice.

- I use basmati rice for all the long-grain rice dishes, as it is similar in flavor to that cooked in Afghanistan.

- Check the rice for any unwanted objects such as stones, and always wash it several times in cold water until it remains clear. This helps to get rid of surplus starch, besides ensuring clean rice.

- Soak the rice for at least half an hour before cooking. Afghans usually prepare and soak their rice for several hours beforehand. The soaking, like the washing, helps to get rid of starch and separates the grains. For *chalau,* some people use the Persian custom of adding a little salt to the water; this helps to whiten the rice.

- Before you put the rice into the boiling water, drain it as thoroughly as possible; and do not stir it too vigorously.

- When using the *sof* method, remember that the parboiling stage takes only 2 to 3 minutes; otherwise the rice will be mushy and sticky.

- For finishing off the rice, to ensure that the grains are separate and fluffy, and have fully absorbed any added flavors, I recommend using a casserole in the oven. It can be done in a tightly covered pan on top of the stove, but do take care to use the lowest possible heat (and perhaps even raise the pan up on a wok ring).

- When Afghans remove rice for serving, they use a *kafgeer.* This large, slotted, flat spoon is used to scrape the rice out very gently, layer by layer. This helps to separate the grains and to keep them from being broken. When the rice is on the serving dish, any lumps are smoothed out by pressing gently with the *kafgeer.*

COOKING SHORT-GRAIN RICE

The basic short-grain rice dish is called *bata*. The rice is cooked with plenty of water until soft and sticky and it is then served with a sauce of some kind.

Shola can be savory or sweet. The savory version is cooked with, or served with, meat and pulses. (The sweet versions are dealt with in the fruits and desserts chapter.) *Ketcheree quroot* is perhaps the most famous short-grain rice dish. It is cooked with *maush* (mung beans) and then served with *qorma* or *kofta,* and with *quroot,* the dried sour yogurt which is reconstituted with water.

MEAT, FISH AND POULTRY

Lamb, beef, veal, goat, water-buffalo and camel are all cooked in Afghanistan, but lamb is the favorite. Because of the Muslim dietary laws, pork is not eaten. The meat eaten by Muslims must be *halal* which means meat, or food, that is lawful. When the animals are slaughtered it must be done in an Islamic fashion, i.e. the animal must be alive before its throat is cut and at the same time the butcher must recite "In the name of God." Then all the blood is drained. *Haram*, on the other hand, means "that which is forbidden," i.e. meat which is not permitted to be eaten such as pork or has not been slaughtered in the correct way.

I should mention here that recipes for some Afghan dishes have not been included in this book as they would be too difficult to make. For example, *landi pilau* is not included. *Landi* is a special type of dried meat. A fat sheep is slaughtered at the end of autumn and the wool is sheared off, leaving the skin with a thick layer of fat underneath. The whole carcase is then hung to dry. Other dried meat, called *gosht-e-qagh,* is also prepared. Drying is done in the summer or early autumn months, when livestock is plentiful, and to ensure that meat is available during the long winter months. The meat (lamb, goat or beef) is cut into chunks and then scored quite deeply in several places. Salt (and sometimes asafoetida) is rubbed in all over it and the meat is then hung up in a warm shady place for about two days to allow it to dry and let the juices drip out. Next the meat is salted some more and for another two or three days left in the sun, after which it is left for four to five days in a warm place but where there is a through draft or a breeze. After that the meat is kept hanging in a cool place, such as a cellar. Before cooking, the dried meat is soaked in warm water for two to three hours and washed several times to get rid of the salt and asafoetida.

Dried meat is used for making soups and stews, in *pilaus*, etc. Travelers carry this dried meat with them on long journeys, to make a simple soup or stew while at the *caravanserai* or wherever they set up camp.

Other dishes I have not included include *cala pilau,* rice cooked with the head *(cala)* and feet *(pacha)* of an animal and a soup, also made from the head and feet of animals, called *sherwa-e-cala pacha*. *Qau* is a whole young lamb roasted in a *tandoor* oven for weddings and special occasions.

Meat is cooked with or without bone. For stews and soups, meat on the bone is preferred as it enhances the flavor and texture of the sauce. Many Afghans like to eat the marrow from a cooked bone.

Poultry, especially chicken, is liked but expensive, so usually reserved for guests and special occasions. Game such as gazelle, ibex, duck, quail, pigeon and partridge, when available, is prized but not readily available.

Afghanistan is landlocked, so sea fish are not a regular part of the diet, but in the winter months some are imported from Pakistan and sold in the bazaars. Shellfish are never eaten. However, many of the rivers teem with fish. Both brown trout and rainbow trout are found. A subspecies of brown trout swims in streams north of the Hindu Kush. This is locally called *mahi-e-khaldar*, which means "spotted fish." *Sheer mahi*, which means "milk fish" is a type of barbel also found in streams both north and south of the Hindu Kush. The name was probably given because of the milky white underbelly of the fish in southern Afghanistan (in the north, it is yellow). This is a tasty fish, although bony and is perhaps the most common all over the country. Carp is also available, from the Daruntah dam near Jalalabad. The most common fish on sale in the bazaars in winter is *mahi laqa,* a large catfish found in the Kunduz river.

PILAU

Yellow Rice Cooked by the *Sof* Method

This basic *pilau* is quick and simple and can be served with a meat or vegetable stew.

    1 lb (2½ cups) white long-grain rice
    2 tsp sugar
    6 tbs water or stock
    4 - 6 tbs vegetable oil
    1 - 2 tsp *char masala* (p. 27) or ground cumin
    salt

Wash the rice several times in cold clean water until it runs clear. Add fresh water and soak the rice for at least half an hour and preferably longer.

Place the sugar in a pan and stir over a medium to high heat until it melts and turns a dark golden brown. Remove the pan from the heat and carefully add the water. Then add the oil, *char masala* and salt. Stir well, and keep warm over a medium to low heat.

Bring 5 cups of water to a boil in a large pan. Add 1 teaspoon of salt. Drain the rice thoroughly and add to the boiling water. Parboil for 2 to 3 minutes. Drain in a large sieve or colander and put in a casserole with a tightly fitting lid.

Pour the sugar mixture over the rice and stir carefully. Cover with the lid and put in a preheated oven at 300°F for about 30 to 45 minutes. Alternatively, the rice can be finished off in a pan over a low heat, for the same length of time.

SERVES 4

PILAU II

Yellow Rice by the *Dampokht* Method

1 lb (2½ cups) white long-grain rice
2 tsp sugar
2 cups water or stock
4 - 6 tbs vegetable oil
1 - 2 tsp *char masala* (p. 27) or ground cumin
salt

Rinse the rice several times in cold water until it remains clear. Add fresh water and soak the rice for at least half an hour and preferably longer.

Place the sugar in a large flameproof casserole and stir over a medium to high heat until the sugar dissolves and turns dark golden brown. Remove from the heat while you add the water or stock, the oil, *char masala* and salt, then bring back to a boil. Drain the rice thoroughly, add it to the boiling liquid (the liquid should cover the rice by about ½ inch) and continue cooking over a medium heat, with the lid on, until the liquid has evaporated and the rice is al dente. Then stir once, very carefully so as not to break the rice, cover with the lid and put in a preheated oven at 300°F for 20 to 30 minutes. Alternatively, the rice can be finished off in a tightly covered pan over a very low heat for the same length of time.

SERVES 4

YAKHNI PILAU
Rice with Boiled Meat

Yakhni is the juice of meat and onions and this *pilau* is often made for people who are ill or sick because the meat and onions are not fried in oil and are therefore easy to digest. If using lamb, trim off excess fat. This recipe uses the *dampokht* method for cooking the rice.

> 1 lb (2½ cups) white long-grain rice, preferably basmati
> 1½ - 2 lbs lamb on the bone or 1 small chicken, cut into pieces
> 2 medium onions, chopped
> 2 oz carrots, chopped into 1-inch pieces
> salt and pepper
> 2 tsp *char masala* (p. 27)
> ¼ tsp saffron (optional)

Rinse the rice several times in cold water until it remains clear. Add fresh water and leave the rice to soak for at least half an hour.

Put the meat in a casserole and cover with 2 cups water. Bring to a boil and skim off any froth which forms. Add the chopped onions and carrots. Sprinkle with the salt and pepper, reduce the heat, and simmer until the meat is tender.

Remove the meat from the casserole and reserve. Strain the stock and measure out 2 cups and put it back into the casserole. Drain the rice well and add it, followed by the meat and vegetables; the rice and meat should be covered by about ½ inch of stock, if not, add a little more water. Add the spices, bring to a boil, cover with a lid, turn down the heat slightly, and boil gently until the rice is tender and the liquid has evaporated. To finish off the rice, place the casserole with the lid on tightly in a preheated oven at 300°F, for 20 to 30 minutes; or leave it in a tightly covered pan on top of the stove, over a very low heat, for the same length of time.

To serve, mound the rice, meat and carrots on to a large dish.

SERVES 4

QABILI PILAU
Yellow Rice with Carrots and Raisins

This *pilau* is probably the best known and could almost be described as Afghanistan's national dish. Any *pilau,* including this one, can be served as a meal on its own or can be served with a *qorma* or vegetable dish. If you use lamb which is fatty, trim off the excess fat, otherwise the *pilau* will be too greasy. This recipe uses the *sof* method of cooking the rice.

    1 lb (2½ cups) long-grain rice,
    preferably basmati
    6 tbs vegetable oil
    2 medium onions, chopped
    1½ - 2 lbs lamb on the bone or 1 chicken, jointed
    salt and pepper
    2 large carrots
    4 oz black seedless raisins
    2 tsp *char masala* (p. 27) or cumin
    ¼ tsp saffron (optional)

Rinse the rice several times in cold water until it remains clear. Add fresh water and leave the rice to soak for at least half an hour, preferably longer.

Heat 4 tablespoons of the vegetable oil in a large pan and add the chopped onions. Stir and fry them until brown. Remove from the oil and add the lamb. Brown well on all sides in the oil. Add about 1 cup of water, and salt and pepper. Bring to a boil, then turn down the heat, cover and simmer until the meat is tender. When cooked, remove the meat and put it in a warm place. Grind the onions to a pulp, add them to the meat broth and stir well. Reserve.

While the meat is cooking, wash and peel the carrots and cut into pieces the size of a matchstick. Heat the remaining 2 table-spoons of oil in a small pan and add the carrots. Cook the carrots gently until they are lightly browned and tender. If they are tough it may be necessary to add a little water and simmer until tender. All the water should evaporate. Remove the carrots from the oil, add the raisins, and cook these gently until they begin to swell up. Remove from the oil and set aside with the carrots. Save any remaining oil for the rice.

Bring 5 cups of water to a boil and add about 1 teaspoon of salt. Drain the rice and add to the boiling water. Parboil for 2 to 3 minutes before draining the rice in a large sieve. Put the rice in a large casserole and sprinkle with the *char masala* and saffron (if used). Take the meat juices and measure out approximately ¾ cup. Pour the juices over the rice and stir very gently once. Then place the cooked meat on one side of the casserole and the carrots and raisins on the other. Add any oil left over from cooking the carrots. Cover with a tightly fitting lid and place in a preheated oven at 300°F for about 45 minutes or leave it in a tightly covered pan on top of the stove over a very low heat for the same length of time.

To serve, remove the carrots and raisins and set to one side. Remove the meat and set to one side. Take about a quarter of the rice and put on a large dish. Top with the meat, then cover with the remaining rice. Garnish the top of the rice with the carrots and raisins.

SERVES 4

QABILI PILAU UZBEKI
Uzbek Rice with Carrots and Raisins

This is *Qabili pilau* as prepared by the Uzbeks using the *dampokht* method of cooking rice. It is, I think, a quicker and simpler way than the *sof* method. The recipe was given to me by Sarah Rashidzada, an Uzbek friend.

　　1 lb (2½ cups) long-grain rice, preferably basmati
　　6 - 8 tbs vegetable oil
　　2 medium onions, chopped
　　1½ lbs lamb on the bone or 1 chicken, jointed
　　salt
　　2 large carrots
　　4 oz raisins
　　2 tsp ground cumin
　　1 tsp black pepper

Rinse the rice several times until the water remains clear, then leave it to soak in fresh water for at least half an hour.

Heat the oil in a flameproof casserole over a medium to high heat and add the chopped onions. Fry until golden brown and soft. Add the meat (if lamb, trimmed of excess fat) and fry until well browned. Then add enough water to cover the meat, and salt, bring to a boil, turn down the heat, and cook gently until the meat is tender.

While the meat is cooking, wash, peel and cut up the carrots into pieces like matchsticks.

When the meat is done and you are ready to cook the rice, add the carrots and the raisins to the top of the meat, sprinkle with 1 teaspoon each of cumin and black pepper, and salt.

Drain the rice, place it on top of the carrots and raisins, and add enough water to cover it by about ½ inch. Add the other teaspoon of cumin and a little salt, bring to a boil, turn down the heat, cover, and boil gently for 10 to 12 minutes until the rice is tender and the water absorbed. (It is important that you listen carefully while cooking this rice for a ticking noise. When you hear it, remove the pan immediately from the heat.)

Place the casserole, which should have a tightly fitting lid, in a preheated oven at 300°F for about 45 minutes. Or you can finish the cooking by leaving it over a very low heat on top of the stove for the same length of time.

To serve, mound the rice, meat, carrots and raisins on a large dish.

SERVES 4

KOFTA PILAU
Yellow Rice and Meatballs

This recipe usea the *sof* method for cooking the rice.

1 lb (2½ cups) long-grain white rice, preferably basmati
Kofta chalau (p. 158)
2 tsp *char masala* (p. 27)
salt

Rinse the rice several times in cold water until it remains clear. Add fresh water and leave the rice to soak for at least half an hour.

Cook the meatballs and sauce as in the recipe for *Kofta chalau* but omitting the yogurt.

Bring 5 cups water to a boil with about 1 teaspoon of salt. Drain the rice and add to the boiling water. Parboil for 2 to 3 minutes. Drain the rice in a large sieve.

Put half of the rice in a large casserole with a tightly fitting lid and then add the meatballs with the rest of the rice on top. Add enough water to the sauce of the meatballs to make ¾ cup, add it to the rice, and sprinkle the *char masala* on top of the rice. Mix gently, taking care not to break the meatballs. Cover and put into a preheated oven at 300°F for about 45 minutes; or leave over a very low heat on top of the stove for the same length of time.

When serving, the meatballs are mixed in with the rice.

Delicious served with a mixed salad or a *burani* dish.

SERVES 4

QORMA PILAU
Yellow Rice and Meat

This recipe uses the *sof* method of cooking rice. If using lamb, trim off excess fat before cooking.

1 lb (2½ cups) long-grain white rice, preferably basmati
6 tbs vegetable oil
2 medium onions, chopped
1½ - 2 lbs lamb on the bone or 1 chicken, jointed
1½ oz yellow split peas
½ tsp ground black cardamom
salt
1 hot green chili or 1 tsp black pepper
1 tsp ground green cardamom seeds
½ tsp saffron, soaked in a little warm water
1 tsp ground cumin

Rinse the rice several times until the water remains clear, and leave it to soak in fresh water for at least half an hour.

Heat the oil in a large pan and fry the chopped onions over a medium to high heat until reddish-brown. Remove the onions and set to one side. Add the meat to the oil and fry until well browned all over. Add the fried onions, split peas and enough water to cover the meat. Add the black cardamom and salt. Cook slowly over a low to medium heat until the meat and peas are tender. Add the chili pepper, the green cardamom and ¼ tsp of the saffron.

Bring 5 cups of salted water to a boil in a large casserole with a tightly fitting lid. Drain the rice, add it to the boiling water, parboil it for 2 to 3 minutes, then drain it again in a large sieve.

Place about half of the rice back in the casserole, add the meat, peas, the remaining saffron, and the ground cumin. Add the rest of the rice on top. Measure out about ¾ cup of meat juices (if the liquid has reduced too much, add extra water) and pour over the rice. Top with a tightly fitting lid and place in a preheated oven at 300°F for about 45 minutes; or leave it over a very low heat on top of the stove for the same length of time.

SERVES 4

BOR PILAU
Rice with Chicken and Yogurt

I like to serve this *pilau* with a *burani* dish or a *qorma*.

1 medium/large onion, finely sliced
6 tbs vegetable oil
1½ lbs boneless chicken or lamb, cut into small chunks
1 - 2 cloves of garlic, peeled and crushed
8 oz yogurt
salt and red pepper
1 tsp ground cilantro seed
1 lb (2½ cups) basmati rice
¼ tsp saffron, soaked in about
1 tbs warm water
1 tsp ground cardamom

Fry the sliced onion in the oil until soft and golden brown. Add the chicken or lamb pieces and fry until golden brown. Add the garlic and fry for a minute or two. Now add the yogurt, salt, red pepper and ground cilantro. Simmer over a medium heat until the meat is tender (about 40 minutes).

Meanwhile wash and soak the rice in plenty of water for about 30 minutes.

Bring 5 cups water to a boil in a large pan and add the rice. Bring back to a boil and cook for 2 to 3 minutes, then strain in a colander. Take one half of the rice and put in a large pan. Add the chicken and its juices. Add the remaining half of the rice and sprinkle the saffron and cardamom and a little more red pepper over it. Cover the pan with a tightly fitting lid and increase the heat for a minute or so to bring back the juices to a boil, then place the pan in a preheated oven at 300°F for about 45 minutes.

SERVES **4**

SHIBIT PILAU
Rice with Dill and Red Raisins

The golden saffron contrasts beautifully with the red raisins and green dill in this dish.

   1 lb (2½ cups) long-grain rice, preferably basmati
   2 medium onions, finely chopped
   6 tbs vegetable oil
   1½ lbs chicken or lamb, preferably on the bone
   salt
   1 tsp black pepper
   2 tbs dill weed
   ½ tsp saffron, soaked in a little warm water
   3 oz (75 g) red raisins

Rinse the rice several times until the water remains clear, then leave to soak in fresh water for at least half an hour.

Fry the onion in the oil until golden brown and soft. Now add the meat cut into serving-size pieces, trimmed of any excess fat. Continue frying until golden brown. Now add enough water to just cover the meat and add salt to taste. Boil gently until the meat is tender.

Bring a large pan of water with about 1 teaspoon of salt to a boil. Drain the rice and add to the boiling water. Boil for about 3 minutes, then drain in a large colander or sieve.

Now place about half of the rice in the pan and top with the meat, reserving the meat juices. Divide the remaining rice into half. Add the first half on top of the meat. Measure out ¾ cup of the meat juices in a bowl or measuring cup and add the black pepper and the dill. Now pour carefully over the rice and meat. To the remaining rice add the saffron, mix gently and place on top of one half of the rice and meat in the pan. To the other side place the raisins. Cover with a tightly fitting lid and place over a high heat to bring the juices in the rice to a boil then quickly place in a preheated oven at 300°F for about half an hour, or a little longer.

To serve, gently remove the raisins from the top of the rice and reserve in a warm place. Repeat this with the saffron rice. Now mound the remaining rice and meat on a large serving platter and then garnish the top with the saffron rice and raisins.

SERVES 4

YAHKOOT PILAU
Rice with Tomatoes

This recipe is a family favorite and easy to make. The tomatoes give the rice a reddish color; hence its name, *yahkoot*, meaning "ruby." If using lamb, trim off excess fat before cooking. I like to serve this with cilantro or mint chutney and yogurt.

1 lb (2½ cups) long-grain white rice, preferably basmati
2 medium onions, chopped
6 tbs vegetable oil
1½ - 2 lbs lamb or chicken on the bone, cut into pieces
2 cloves garlic, peeled and crushed
1 tsp turmeric
1 can (14 oz) chopped tomatoes
1 tsp sugar
salt and pepper
1 tsp ground green cardamom seeds

Measure out the rice and rinse several times until the water remains clear. Add fresh water and leave the rice to soak for at least half an hour.

Fry the chopped onions in the oil, in a large casserole with a tightly fitting lid, until reddish-brown, then add the meat, crushed garlic and turmeric. Fry until the meat is well browned. Add the tomatoes, sugar, salt and pepper. Stir well, bring to a boil, then turn down the heat and cook until the meat is tender.

Drain the rice and add it to the cooked meat and juices. Add enough water to cover the rice and the meat by about ½ inch. Sprinkle in the ground cardamom and stir gently. Bring to a boil,

cover with the lid, turn down the heat to medium/low and cook
for 10 to 15 minutes until the rice is tender and all the liquid has
evaporated. If the liquid has evaporated and the rice is still not
cooked, add a little more water and cook until the additional
water has been absorbed. Cover with the lid and put in a preheated oven at 300°F for 20 to 30 minutes. The rice could also be
cooked over a very low flame or heat for the same length of time,
if preferred.

To serve, mound the rice and meat on a large warm serving
dish.

SERVES 4

BONJON PILAU
Yellow Rice with Eggplant

This is a rich and spicy *pilau*. The *sof* method is used for cooking
the rice.

    1 lb (2½ cups) long-grain white rice, preferably basmati
    2 medium/large (1 lb) eggplants
    10 tbs vegetable oil
    2 medium onions, chopped
    1½ - 2 lbs lamb or beef on the bone, cut into pieces
    2 cloves garlic, peeled and crushed
    salt and black or red pepper
    1 tsp turmeric
    1 tsp ground cilantro
    ½ tsp saffron

Rinse the rice several times until the water remains clear, then
leave it to soak in fresh water for at least half an hour.

Peel and slice the eggplants lengthwise to about ½ inch thickness. Heat 4 tablespoons of the oil in a pan and fry the chopped
onions over medium heat until golden brown and soft, then put in
the meat (if lamb, trimmed of excess fat) and fry until well

browned, stirring frequently. Add 1 cup water, salt and pepper, and bring to a boil. Stir, then lower the heat and cook until the meat is tender.

Meanwhile heat the remaining 6 tablespoons oil in a large frying pan and fry the eggplants on both sides until golden. You may need a little more oil as they tend to soak it up during cooking, but drain them thoroughly on absorbent paper otherwise the rice will be too oily. Reserve the eggplants.

Mix the garlic, turmeric and cilantro together in a little water and add to the eggplant. Add to this ¾ cup of juices from the meat and simmer over a low heat for about half an hour.

Bring 5 cups salted water to a boil. Drain the rice, put it into the boiling water, parboil it for 2 to 3 minutes, then drain it in a large sieve. Next, put half the rice in a large casserole which has a tightly fitting lid, and add the meat.

Sprinkle with red or black pepper, according to taste, cover with a little more of the rice, add the eggplants, then top with the remaining rice. Add the saffron to the remaining juices from the meat and eggplants and pour over the rice. Cover with the lid and put in a preheated oven at 300°F for about 45 minutes; or leave it over a very low heat on top of the stove for the same length of time.

To serve, remove the top layer of rice and place on a warm dish. Cover with the meat and eggplants and then add the remaining rice.

SERVES 4

ZAMARUD or SABZI PILAU

Rice with Spinach

A beautiful green dish; *zamarud* means "emerald."

1 lb (2½ cups) long-grain white rice, preferably basmati
1½ - 2 lbs lamb on the bone, or 1 chicken, jointed
8 tbs vegetable oil
2 medium onions, chopped
2 tsp *char masala* (p. 27)
salt and black pepper
1 lb spinach
4 oz leeks or *gandana* (p. 34)
2 tsp powdered dill weed or ground cilantro
1 or 2 hot green chilies

Rinse the rice several times until the water remains clear, then leave it to soak in fresh water for at least half an hour.

If using lamb trim off excess fat. Heat 6 tablespoons of the oil in a pan and fry the onions in it, stirring frequently until golden brown and soft. Add the lamb or chicken and continue frying until the meat and onions are well browned. Next, add 1 cup water, 1 teaspoon of the *char masala*, salt and plenty of black pepper, bring to a boil, turn down the heat, stir well, and simmer until the meat is tender.

Now prepare the spinach as for *sabzi chalau* (p. 162). Wash and thoroughly drain the spinach. Cut the leeks into small pieces and wash thoroughly. Chop up the spinach. Heat the remaining 2 tablespoons oil in a large pan and fry the leeks in it, until they are soft and nearly brown, then add the spinach and continue to fry, stirring continuously, until it reduces in size. Reduce the heat, cover the pan, and simmer until the spinach is cooked. Then add the dill, salt and pepper, cover again and continue to cook gently until all water has evaporated and the spinach is creamy and soft.

Bring 5 cups of water to a boil with about 1 teaspoon of salt, drain the rice and put it in the boiling water. Parboil it for 2 to 3 minutes, then drain it in a large sieve and transfer it to a large casserole with a tightly fitting lid. Add the cooked spinach, the meat with about ¾ cup of the juices and 1 teaspoon of *char masala*. Mix gently but thoroughly. Place the hot chilies on top of the rice, cover and put in a preheated oven at 300°F for about 45 minutes.

To serve, remove the chilies from the top of the rice and reserve, then carefully mound the rice and meat on a large serving platter. Garnish with the chilies.

SERVES **4**

SAMARUQ PILAU
Rice with Mushrooms

Large flat mushrooms used for stuffing are good for this dish. They have the right meatiness and texture. This *pilau* can also be prepared without any meat in which case increase the amount of mushrooms accordingly.

1 lb (2½ cups) long-grain rice, preferably basmati
8 tbs vegetable oil
1 large onion, finely chopped
1 lb chicken or lamb, preferably on the bone,
    cut into serving-sized portions
1 can (14 oz) chopped tomatoes
salt
12 oz mushrooms, cut into ¾-inch cubes
1 tsp black pepper
1 tsp ground cardamom

Wash and rinse the rice until the water becomes clear, then soak for about half an hour in plenty of water.

With 4 tablespoons of the oil, fry the onions over a medium/high until golden brown. Now add the meat and continue frying until browning. Add the tomatoes and salt to taste and boil gently until the meat is tender.

Meanwhile, with the other 4 tablespoons of oil, fry the mushrooms coating them well. Add the mushrooms to the meat and tomatoes. Drain the rice and also add to the pan. Now add enough water to cover the meat, rice and tomato by about ½ inch. Add salt, black pepper and the cardamom. Bring to a boil, then cover with a tightly fitting lid and turn down the heat to low/medium for 10 to 15 minutes. When all the liquid has evaporated, stir gently to mix the ingredients, cover again with the lid and place in a preheated oven at 300°F for about 30 minutes or a little longer.

SERVES 4

MAUSH PILAU
Rice, Mung Beans and Apricots or Dates

This *pilau* is often cooked without meat. The apricots or dates make an unusual but delicious addition. If using lamb, trim off excess fat before cooking. The *sof* method of cooking rice is used here.

5 oz mung beans
5 oz dried apricots or dates
1 lb (2½ cups) long-grain white rice, preferably basmati
½ cup vegetable oil
2 medium onions, chopped
2 lbs lamb or beef on the bone, cut into pieces
salt and pepper
2 tsp ground cumin or *char masala* (p. 27)

Wash the mung beans and leave them to soak for 1 to 2 hours. Cook the apricots or dates in a little water until they are just soft and reserve.

Rinse the rice several times until the water remains clear, and leave it to soak in fresh water for at least half an hour. Heat the oil in a pan and fry the onions until brown. Remove the onions and add the meat and brown well in the oil. Add 1 cup water, and salt and pepper, bring to a boil, then turn down the heat, cover, and cook gently until the meat is tender. When cooked, remove the meat and set aside in a warm place. Grind the browned onions to a pulp and add to the meat juices, stirring well.

Bring 6 cups water to boil in a large casserole and add the mung beans. Cook them until half done (10 to 15 minutes). Then drain the rice and add it to the mung beans. Bring back to a boil, add salt and boil for 2 to 3 minutes. Drain the rice and mung beans in a large sieve, then return to the casserole. Sprinkle with the cumin and add 1 cup of the meat juices. Place the meat on top of one side of the rice and the apricots or dates on the other side. Cover tightly and put in a preheated oven at 300°F for about 45 minutes; or leave over a very low heat on top of the stove for the same length of time.

Serve the meat on a large dish, topped with the rice and mung beans and garnish with the apricots or dates.

SERVES 6

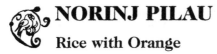

NORINJ PILAU
Rice with Orange

Traditionally this *pilau* is prepared with the peel of bitter (or Seville) oranges *(norinj)*. It is quite a sweet dish. My family in Afghanistan made this slightly different recipe which is not so sweet and I much prefer it. I have also used the peel of ordinary oranges which are easier to obtain. *Norinj pilau* is one of my favorite Afghan dishes and it has a lovely delicate flavor. This recipe uses the *dampokht* method of cooking rice. If using lamb, trim off excess fat.

> 1 lb (2½ cups) long-grain white rice, preferably basmati
> 6 tbs vegetable oil
> 2 medium onions, chopped
> 1 medium chicken or 1½ - 2 lbs lamb on the bone, cut in pieces
> salt and pepper
> peel of 1 large orange
> ¼ cup sugar
> 1 - 2 tbs blanched and slivered almonds
> 1 - 2 tbs blanched and slivered pistachios
> ½ tsp saffron
> 1 - 2 tbs rosewater
> 1 tsp ground green cardamom seeds

Measure out the rice and rinse several times until the water remains clear. Add fresh water and leave the rice to soak for at least half an hour.

Heat the oil and add the chopped onions. Stir and fry them over a medium to high heat until golden brown and soft. Add the meat and fry until brown, turning frequently. Add 2 cups water, salt and pepper and cook gently until the meat is tender.

While the meat is cooking, wash and cut up the peel of 1 large orange into matchstick-size pieces, removing as much pith as possible. To remove any bitter taste, put the orange strips into a strainer and dip first in boiling water and then cold. Repeat this several times. Set aside.

Make a syrup by bringing to a boil ½ cup water and the sugar. Add the orange peel, the almonds and pistachios to the boiling syrup. Boil for about 5 minutes, skimming off the thick froth when necessary. Strain and set aside the peel and nuts. Add the saffron and rosewater to the syrup and boil again gently for another 3 minutes. Add the ground cardamom.

To cook the rice, strain and reserve the chicken stock (setting the meat to one side). Combine the syrup and stock to make 2 cups liquid, adding extra water if necessary. The oil will be on the surface of the stock and this should also be included in the cooking of the rice. Bring the liquid to a boil in a large casserole. Drain the rice and then add it to the boiling liquid. Add salt, the nuts and the peel, reserving about a third for garnishing. Bring back to a boil, then cover with a tightly fitting lid, turn down the heat to medium and boil for about 10 minutes until the rice is tender and all the liquid is absorbed.

Add the meat, the remaining peel and nuts on top of the rice and cover with the tightly fitting lid. Put into a preheated oven at 300°F for 20 to 30 minutes; or cook over a very low heat for the same length of time.

When serving, place the meat in the center of a large dish, mound the rice over the top and then garnish with the orange peel and nuts.

SERVES 4

ZARDA PILAU
Yellow Rice, Nuts and Saffron

The saffron gives the rice a yellow color, hence its name, *zard* meaning "yellow." It is usually only prepared for guests or for special occasions. If using lamb, trim off excess fat. This recipe uses the *sof* method of cooking rice.

> 1 lb (2½ cups) long-grain white rice, preferably basmati
> 6 tbs vegetable oil
> 2 medium onions, chopped
> 1½ - 2 lbs lamb on the bone, or 1 chicken, cut in pieces
> salt and pepper
> ¼ cup sugar
> 2 tbs pistachios, skinned and slivered
> 2 tbs almonds, skinned and slivered
> ½ tsp saffron
> 2 tsp *char masala* (p. 27)

Rinse the rice several times until the water remains clear. Add fresh water and leave the rice to soak for at least half an hour, preferably longer.

Heat the vegetable oil in a large casserole and add the chopped onions. Stir and fry until they are golden brown. Add the lamb or chicken and brown well on all sides. Add about 1 cup water and salt and pepper, Cover and bring to a boil, then turn down the heat and simmer until the meat is tender. Remove the meat and set aside, preferably in a warm place.

Shortly before you are ready to cook the rice, make a syrup with ½ cup water and the sugar. Put them in a pan and bring to a boil. Boil until syrupy (about 5 minutes). Add the pistachios, almonds and saffron. Keep warm.

Bring 5 cups water and 1 teaspoon salt to a boil. Drain the rice and put into the boiling water. Parboil the rice for 2 to 3 minutes. Drain it in a large sieve. Mix gently approximately one quarter of the rice into the warm syrup. Put the remaining rice in a large casserole, sprinkle with the *char masala*.

Measure out approximately ¾ cup of the meat juices and pour them over the rice. Top the rice on one side with the meat and put the rice containing the nuts on the other side. Cover with a tightly fitting lid. Put the casserole into a preheated oven at 300°F for about 45 minutes, or cook over a very low heat for the same length of time, if you prefer.

To serve, remove the meat and set to one side. Next remove the rice containing the nuts and set aside. Then take about one quarter of the remaining rice and put on a large dish. Top with the meat, then cover with the remaining rice. Garnish the top with the nuts mixed with rice.

SERVES 4

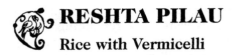

RESHTA PILAU
Rice with Vermicelli

Reshta in Dari means "thread." In Afghanistan, *reshta pilau* is sometimes a sweet *pilau* made with fine egg vermicelli. This recipe does not contain meat but it can be eaten with a stew (*qorma*) or vegetable dish.

    1 lb (2½ cups) long-grain white rice, preferably basmati
    salt
    ½ cup vegetable oil
    8 oz fine egg vermicelli, broken into lengths
        of about 1 inch
    1 cup sugar
    ½ tsp saffron
    2 tbs pistachios, skinned and cut into quarters
    2 tbs almonds, skinned and cut into quarters

Wash the rice several times in water until the color remains clear. Soak the rice in fresh water for at least half an hour, preferably longer.

Bring 5 cups water to a boil in a large casserole and add about 1 teaspoon of salt. Drain the rice thoroughly and add to the boiling water. Parboil the rice for 2 to 3 minutes. Drain it in a large sieve. Take three quarters of the rice and put into a large casserole covered with a tightly fitting lid. Keep in a warm place. Reserve the remaining quarter of the rice.

Heat ¼ cup of the vegetable oil in a pan over a medium heat and add the egg vermicelli. Fry gently for a few minutes. Do not brown.

Put 1 cup water in another pan and add the sugar. Bring to a boil and stir over a high heat until a thin syrup forms (about 5 minutes). Add the fried vermicelli, saffron and nuts to this syrup.

Take a large spoonful of the reserved rice and put in a sieve. Add a large spoonful of the vermicelli mixed with syrup. Repeat, layering in this way until all the rice and vermicelli are in the sieve.

Now assemble the various preparations before the final cooking. Mix together 6 tablespoons water, the remaining ¼ cup oil and salt. Add this to the rice in the casserole, stir once gently and then place the rice and vermicelli mixture from the sieve on top of one side of the plain rice. Do not stir. Cover with the tightly fitting lid and place in a preheated oven at 300°F for about 45 minutes.

To serve, first remove and reserve the rice and vermicelli mixture and then place the plain rice on a large dish. Garnish the rice with the vermicelli, sweetened rice and nuts.

SERVES 4

🐚 RESHTA PILAU II
Rice with Vermicelli

I find this method of cooking *reshta pilau* much easier than the previous recipe; it contains meat and is not so sweet.

1 medium onion, finely chopped
8 tablespoons vegetable oil
1½ lbs boneless lamb or chicken, cut into cubes
salt and pepper
½ tsp cinnamon
1 lb (2½ cups) long-grain rice, preferably basmati
4 oz fine vermicelli, broken into lengths of about 1 inch
4 tbs green or red raisins
2 tbs pistachio, skinned and slivered
2 tbs almonds, skinned and slivered
¼ tsp saffron, soaked in 1 tbs hot water
1 tbs rosewater

Fry the onion over a medium heat in about 5 tablespoons oil until golden brown and soft, then add the lamb or chicken. Fry until golden brown. Add the salt, pepper and cinnamon. Add water to just cover the meat and bring to a boil. Then turn down the heat and simmer until the meat is tender and the juices are reduced and thickened. (This takes about 45 minutes to 1 hour).

Rinse the rice several times in water then leave to soak in cold water for about half an hour.

Meanwhile, gently fry the vermicelli in 2 tablespoons of oil for a few minutes until golden brown. Reserve. In the remaining 1 tablespoon of oil, now fry the raisins and nuts for a couple of minutes, stirring well.

Bring a large pot of water to a boil, then drain the rice and add to the boiling water along with the reserved vermicelli. Boil for about 3 minutes then strain in a large sieve or colander.

Add half the rice and vermicelli to a large casserole or pan with a tightly fitting lid, then add the cooked meat and about ¾ cup of the juices. Top with half the remaining rice. To the other half add the liquid saffron and the rosewater. Mix gently and place on top of the rice in the pan on one side. On the other side add the nuts and raisins. Cover the pan with a lid and place in a preheated oven at 300°F for about 45 minutes to 1 hour.

To serve, first remove the saffron rice and the nuts and raisins and set to one side in a warm place. Then place half the rice on a large serving dish, top with the meat, then add the remaining rice on top. Decorate the top of the rice with the saffron rice, nuts and raisins.

SERVES **4**

PILAU-E-MURGH-E-SHEKAM PUR
Rice with Stuffed Chicken

This is an elaborate recipe and is only prepared in Afghanistan for very special occasions. It is quite complicated and you will need a large deep casserole for this dish as the chicken is cooked whole in the rice.

FOR THE STUFFING:
2 oz yellow split peas
peel of 2 oranges
1 cup red raisins
1 cup almonds and pistachios, blanched and chopped
2 tbs vegetable oil
4 oz minced lamb
salt and pepper
½ tsp ground green cardamom

FOR THE *PILAU*:
6 tbs vegetable oil
1 medium/large onion, shredded or grated
1 medium chicken
4 whole cardamom pods
salt and pepper
1½ lbs (3¾ cups) long-grain rice, preferably basmati
1 tsp ground cinnamon
1 tsp ground cumin
½ tsp saffron, soaked in a little warm water

TO PREPARE THE STUFFING: Wash the split peas and leave to soak in warm water for about an hour, then boil them in plenty of water until soft.

Peel the orange, removing as much pith as possible (I find it easier to use a potato peeler to do this) and cut into match-stick size strips. To remove any bitter taste, put the orange strips into a strainer and dip first in boiling water and then cold water. Repeat this several times, then set aside.

Now fry the raisins, almonds and pistachios in the oil for a couple of minutes. Remove and set to one side. Now fry the lamb in the same oil until brown. Remove and set to one side to cool.

TO PREPARE THE *PILAU*: In 4 tablespoons of the oil fry the shredded or grated onion until brown and a little crisp. Remove and pound or grind in a pestle and mortar. Leave to one side. In the remaining 2 tablespoons oil fry the chicken whole in a casserole, browning on all sides. When nicely brown, add the reserved onion, the whole cardamom pods and water to just cover the chicken. Add salt and pepper. Bring to a boil and then cook gently until the chicken is just tender, about 40 to 45 minutes. Do not overcook or the chicken will fall to pieces when you remove it from the broth and will be difficult to stuff.

While the chicken is cooking prepare the rice by rinsing several times in cold water and then leaving to soak in fresh water for about half an hour or so.

When the chicken is cooked, remove carefully from the broth and allow to cool a little. Measure out about 1 cup of this broth and stir in the cinnamon and cumin. Set to one side. Now mix together the reserved almonds, pistachios, raisins, orange peel, minced lamb and split peas. Season with salt and pepper and also mix in the ground cardamom. Take half of this mixture and stuff the chicken. Brush the chicken with a little of the diluted saffron.

Bring plenty of salted water to a boil in a large pan and then add the rice. Boil for 2 to 3 minutes until half cooked then drain it in a large sieve or colander.

Take about half of the rice and spread a layer over the bottom of a deep ovenproof casserole. Place the chicken on top and cover with half of the remaining rice. Pour the reserved chicken broth on top. Sprinkle the diluted saffron on the other half of the remaining rice. Add this as a final layer on top of the rice on one side of the casserole and on the other side put the reserved nut mixture. Cover with a tightly fitting lid and place on high heat for a couple of minutes to bring the juices to a boil, then put in a pre-heated oven at 300°F for 45 minutes to 1 hour.

To serve, remove the saffron rice and the nuts and set to one side, keeping warm. Remove the next layer of rice and place on a large serving dish, then carefully remove the chicken and put on top. Then cover with the last layer of rice. Now decorate the whole with the saffron rice and the nuts.

SERVES 6

CHALAU SOF
Plain White Long-grain Rice

Chalau is usually served with a meat or vegetable stew, *qorma,* or meatballs, *kofta.* The basic method for cooking *chalau* the *sof* way is as follows.

1 lb (2½ cups) white long-grain rice
salt
¼ cup vegetable oil
1 tsp ground or whole cumin, or *char masala* (p. 27)

Wash the rice several times until the water remains clear. Soak the rice in water for at least half an hour, preferably longer.

Bring the 5 cups water to a boil in a large pan. Add salt. Drain the rice and add it to the boiling water. Parboil the rice for 2 to 3 minutes. (If you overcook the rice at this stage, the grains will stick together.) Drain the rice in a large sieve or colander and then place the rice in a pan or casserole which has a tightly fitting lid. Mix the oil, 6 tablespoons water, the cumin and salt together and gently pour over the rice. Stir in carefully. Cover with the lid and either place in a preheated oven at 300°F or over a low heat for 30 to 45 minutes.

SERVES 4

 # CHALAU DAMPOKHT

To cook *chalau* by the *dampokht* method you need exactly the same ingredients as for the *sof* method (see preceding recipe) except that 2 cups of water will be enough.

Bring the 2 cups water to a boil in a large pan. Drain the rice as much as possible and add to the boiling water (the rice should be covered by the water by about ½ inch). Add the salt, vegetable oil and cumin. Bring back to a boil, stir gently once, then cover with the lid and turn the heat down to medium. Boil gently until the rice is al dente and all the water has evaporated, this usually takes about 10 minutes. (There will be a ticking noise as the rice catches at the bottom of the pan.) Then put the pan either in a preheated oven at 300°F or over a very low heat on top of the stove for 20 to 30 minutes.

SERVES 4

CHALAU-E-SHIBIT
White Rice with Dill

Serve this *chalau* with kebabs and yogurt, or alternatively with one of the *burani* recipes.

    1 lb (2½ cups) basmati rice
    ¼ cup vegetable oil
    1 tbs dill weed
    6 tbs water or stock
    salt

Prepare and cook as for *chalau sof* (p. 154) or *dampokht* (p. 155) but at the stage when you add the spices, add in the dill.

SERVES **4**

QORMA CHALAU
Meat Stew with Rice

There are many varied *qormas* in Afghanistan, some of them without meat, and here I just give the most usual one served with *chalau*. For other *qormas*, see pages 176–184).

Instead of split peas, other pulses such as red kidney beans may be used (soaked overnight and well cooked before being added to the meat). Or substitute fresh vegetables, such as potatoes, carrots, cauliflower, peas, or green beans, all sliced or diced, added to the *qorma* when the meat is already tender and the sauce thick, and then cook for about 15 minutes, adding a little extra water if necessary.

    6 tbs vegetable oil
    4 medium onions, finely chopped
    2 lbs lamb on the bone, or beef or chicken, cut in pieces
    1 - 2 tbs tomato puree
    2 oz split peas
    1 tsp *char masala* (p. 27) or ground cilantro
    ½ tsp black pepper
    pinch red pepper (optional)
    salt

Heat the oil in a pan and add the chopped onions. Fry over a medium to high heat, stirring frequently until golden brown and soft. Add the meat and fry again until the meat and onions are well browned. Mix in the tomato puree and continue frying for a minute or two. Add ½ cup water, the split peas, *char masala*, peppers and salt and bring to a boil, then turn the heat down and simmer until the meat is cooked and the split peas soft. Add a little more water if necessary. The sauce should be thick and oily, but excess oil can be spooned off if wished. Serve with *chalau* (p. 154) and garnish the rice with a little of the sauce.

SERVES 4

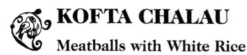

KOFTA CHALAU
Meatballs with White Rice

The word *kofta* derives from the Persian *koofteh*, meaning "pounded meat," which in turn came from the verb *koobidand*, "to pound." *Kofta* come in all kinds of variations (and spellings) throughout the Middle East, Central Asia, the Balkans, India and North Africa. The range includes rissoles, meatballs, croquettes and dumplings which are usually made with ground or mashed meat, well kneaded and often mixed with other ingredients to form a smooth paste. Many have stuffings such as nuts or cheese. See *nargis kebab* (p. 104) for a *kofta* with hard-boiled egg as a stuffing.

Kofta chalau in Afghanistan is a favorite dish. The recipe for the meatballs can also be used with *ketcheree quroot, maushawa* and *aush*.

FOR THE MEATBALLS:
1 lb minced beef or lamb
1 medium onion, minced or ground
2 cloves garlic, peeled and crushed
1 egg
2 tsp ground cilantro
1 tsp *char masala* (p. 27)
½ tsp black pepper
1 tbs finely chopped fresh cilantro

FOR THE SAUCE:
6 tbs vegetable oil
2 medium onions, finely chopped
1 tbs tomato puree
salt
red or black pepper
4 oz (½ cup) yogurt (optional)

Combine and mix together all the ingredients for the meatballs and knead the mixture with the hands until it becomes smooth and sticky. It is essential that the mixture be really well mixed and kneaded to give the meatballs their characteristic smooth texture and also to prevent them from breaking up while being cooked. Shape into balls 1 to 2 inches in diameter. It is best to use wet hands to form the balls into smooth shapes by dipping them from time to time into a little salted water. Some Afghans use egg white to smooth the balls into shape. This also helps prevent the meatball from breaking up.

Heat the oil in a pan over a medium to high heat. Add the chopped onions and fry, stirring continuously until they are red-dish-brown. Add the tomato puree and stir and fry briskly until the sauce turns brownish. Stir in a little water. Add salt and pepper, according to taste. Bring to the boiling point and then add the meatballs, one at a time, in a single layer. Add more water as necessary to just cover the meatballs. Cover with a lid leaving it slightly ajar. Turn down the heat to low and simmer gently for 45 minutes to 1 hour or until the meatballs and sauce are brown and the sauce thick. Carefully stir in the yogurt, if using.

Serve with *chalau*. *Chutni murch* (p. 215) or *chutni gashneez* (p. 213) go particularly well with this dish.

SERVES 4

LAWANG CHALAU
Meat Stew with Yogurt and White Rice

Lawang is a term used to denote any dish to which yogurt is added to the meat or vegetables just before the end of cooking. In this recipe chicken can be substituted for the lamb, if wished. Also turmeric can be used instead of saffron.

    1 large onion, peeled and finely sliced
    1 clove garlic, peeled and crushed
    ¼ cup vegetable oil
    1 lb boneless lamb, cut into serving-size pieces
    1 tbs tomato puree
    ½ tsp saffron (optional)
    2 whole cardamom pods
    salt and pepper
    6 oz (¾ cup) yogurt (*chaka*, see p. 40)

Fry the finely sliced onions and crushed garlic in the oil until soft and golden brown. Add the meat and fry until browning. Add the tomato puree, stir in well and continue frying for about a minute, then add about ½ cup water. Add the saffron, the whole cardamom pods and season with salt and pepper. Bring to a boil, then reduce the heat to medium and cook until the meat is tender. Ten minutes before serving add the yogurt and heat through very gently.
    Serve with *chalau*.

SERVES **4** ·

MAHI CHALAU
Fish Stew with Rice

The large river fish, *mahi laqa,* found in the Kunduz river and used for this dish, is similar in taste and texture to cod or haddock, either of which can be substituted in this recipe. Traditionally, *mooli safaid* (a long white radish, see p. 35) is cooked with the fish (it is considered a "cold" food and balances the fish which is considered "hot"). I have, however, prepared this dish without the *mooli* and it is still very good.

2 lbs fish (see above)
6 tbs vegetable oil
2 lbs *mooli*
1 tsp turmeric
7 oz onions, chopped
3 cloves garlic, peeled and crushed
1 can (14 oz) chopped tomatoes
½ tsp ground cilantro
red pepper
salt

Cut the fish into large chunks. Pat dry with paper towels. Heat the oil in a pan and fry the fish quickly over a high heat on both sides until golden brown. Do not cook through. Remove the fish from the pan and set to one side.

Slice the *mooli* into thin rounds. Bring some water to a boil in a pan, add the *mooli* and ½ tsp of the turmeric. Boil gently until soft, then drain and set to one side.

Filter the oil and put into a deep pan. Heat the oil again and fry the chopped onions and crushed garlic over a medium to high heat until soft and reddish-brown. Mix in the tomatoes and fry vigorously until the tomatoes brown and the liquid reduces. Add a little more than 1 cup water, the cilantro, ½ tsp turmeric, red pepper and salt. Stir, cover, turn down the heat and simmer for about half an hour.

Meanwhile, take half of the *mooli* and place in the bottom of a pan. Add the fish, then top with the remaining *mooli.*

When the tomato sauce is ready pour over the fish and the *mooli* and simmer for a further 15 to 20 minutes. Do not overcook or boil vigorously, or the fish will disintegrate.

Serve with *chalau* (or with *bata,* p. 167).

SERVES 4

SABZI CHALAU
Spinach with Rice

This was one of my mother-in-law's favorite dishes. It can be accompanied by meat in the form of a separately cooked *qorma,* which can be either served separately or added to the spinach just before serving. *Qorma chalau* (p. 157) without the tomato paste would be suitable. The rice is also served on a separate platter.

If the dish is made with short-grain rice, it becomes *Sabzi bata,* as explained on p. 168.

2 lbs spinach
8 oz leeks or *gandana* (p. 34) or scallions
6 tbs vegetable oil
½ tbs fenugreek (optional)
1 tsp ground cilantro (optional)
1 tbs powdered dill weed or 2 tbs fresh cilantro,
    finely chopped
1 tbs lemon juice (optional)
salt and black pepper
1 green chili (optional)

Chop the spinach into small pieces and wash thoroughly. Drain well. Cut up the leeks into small pieces and wash carefully.

Heat the oil and fry the fenugreek (if used) for a minute or so then add the leeks in it until soft and nearly brown. Add the spinach and continue to fry, stirring continuously until it reduces. Then turn the heat down, cover the pan with a lid, and simmer until the spinach is cooked and the oil comes to the surface, about

10 to 15 minutes. At this stage, add the ground cilantro, dill, lemon juice, if used, salt and plenty of black pepper and the chili if used. Cover again and cook until any excess water has evaporated and the spinach becomes creamy and soft. If you are mixing with a meat *qorma*, add it at this stage. Cook for a little longer until the flavors have developed.

Serve with *chalau*.

SERVES 4

ZAMARUD CHALAU
Emerald (spinach) Rice

This recipe differs from *sabzi chalau* (p. 162) in that the rice is actually cooked in the spinach water. This gives the rice a green color and its name, *zamarud,* meaning "emerald." This was one of my favorites when I lived in Afghanistan. It can be served with *kofta* or a *qorma*.

1 lb (2½ cups) long-grain white rice, preferably basmati
2 lbs spinach
8 tbs vegetable oil
8 oz leeks, scallions, or *gandana* (p. 34)
1 tbs dried dill weed or 2 tbs finely chopped fresh cilantro
½ tbs fenugreek (optional)
salt and black pepper
2 tsp cumin, whole or ground

Rinse the rice several times in cold water until it remains clear. Add fresh water and leave the rice to soak for at least half an hour.

Chop the spinach into small pieces and then wash thoroughly. Drain well. Put the spinach into a large pan and add ½ cup water. Add 4 tablespoons of the oil. Put on a medium to high heat and boil for about 5 minutes, stirring occasionally until the spinach reduces and the water becomes green. Drain off the water and oil from the spinach into a bowl or measuring cup, reserving just a little more than half a cup of the juices for cooking the rice.

Chop up the leeks into small pieces and wash thoroughly. Heat the 4 tablespoons of remaining oil in a pan and add the leeks, which should be well drained. Fry over a medium heat until soft but not brown. Add the leeks to the spinach, then add the dill, fenugreek (if used) and salt and pepper. Cook on a low heat, adding any remaining spinach water (except the reserved liquid for cooking the rice), until all the water has evaporated and the spinach is soft.

Remove 2 to 4 tablespoons of the spinach and chop up very fine. Reserve.

Bring 5 cups water to a boil. Drain the rice and add to the boiling water. Parboil for 2 to 3 minutes, then drain the rice in a colander or large sieve. Put the rice in a casserole which has a tightly fitting lid. Now add the reserved cooked spinach, cumin, salt and pepper to the reserved half of cup of spinach juices and stir gently into the rice. Cover with the lid and put in a preheated oven at 300°F for 30 to 45 minutes. Alternatively, cook over a low heat for the same time.

Serve the rice with the spinach and perhaps a *qorma* or salad dish, if desired.

SERVES 4

YAHKOOT CHALAU
Cherry Stew with Rice

Yahkoot means "ruby" in Dari. The cherries symbolize red rubies in this *qorma* and contrast beautifully with the white rice. Sour cherries called *olu bolu* are normally used (see p. 36). However, if you cannot find them you can substitute morello cherries or ordinary dark red cherries but reduce or completely omit the sugar and add a good squeeze of lemon juice, according to taste. Also when cooking the *chalau*, substitute 1 tsp of ground cardamom for the cumin or *char masala*.

2 medium onions, finely sliced
¼ cup vegetable oil
2 lbs lamb or chicken on the bone
3 whole green cardamom pods
½ tsp ground ginger (optional)
salt and red pepper
1 lb dark red cherries, stoned and cut in half
¼ cup sugar
lemon juice (optional)

Fry the onions in the oil until soft and golden brown. Add the meat and continue frying until browning. Add 4 to 6 tablespoons water, the whole cardamom pods, ginger and salt and pepper and cook gently until the meat is tender. Add the cherries and the sugar with a little more water and a squeeze of lemon juice, if desired. Simmer until the cherries are cooked and the flavors well blended, about 15 minutes.
Serve with *chalau*.

SERVES 4

BONJON CHALAU
Eggplant Stew with Rice

This is very similar to ratatouille. Although commonly served with *chalau,* it can also be served with *bata* (p. 167).

> 1 lb eggplants
> 10 tbs vegetable oil
> 1 medium onion, chopped
> 10 tbs tomato juice
> 1 tsp ground cilantro
> salt
> red or black pepper

Peel and chop the eggplants into 1-inch cubes.

Heat the vegetable oil in a pan and add the chopped onion. Fry over a medium to high heat until brown. Remove from the oil and set to one side.

Fry the eggplants in the remaining oil until well browned on all sides. (You may need a little more oil as eggplants soak up a lot.) Grind the fried onions to a pulp in a pestle and mortar and add them to the eggplants. Mix in the tomato juice, ½ cup water, the cilantro, salt and pepper, and then cook gently for about an hour, either on top of the stove in a pan with a tightly fitting lid or in a casserole in a preheated oven at 300°F.

Serve with *chalau.* Some people add yogurt to this dish or serve a bowl of yogurt separately.

SERVES **4**

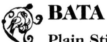

SHALGHAM CHALAU
Turnip Stew with Long-Grain Rice

Cook the turnip stew as in *shalgham bata* (p. 168), but serve it with *chalau* instead of *bata*.

SERVES 4

BATA
Plain Sticky Short-grain Rice

This is the basic short-grain rice dish. It is served with a variety of stews or vegetables the most common being turnip stew, *shalgam bata* (see recipe on p. 168).

1 lb (2 cups) short-grain rice
salt
⅓ cup vegetable oil

Wash the rice and put in a pan with 5 cups of water. Add salt. Bring to a boil, then turn down the heat and cook gently, adding more water if necessary, until the rice is soft and the water evaporated, about 20 to 30 minutes. Stir from time to time to prevent sticking. Cover with a tightly fitting lid and put in an oven preheated at 300°F or cook over a low heat for half an hour. Then stir the rice; it should be thick and sticky. Add the oil, cover with the lid, and cook for a further half an hour.

SERVES 4

BONJON BATA

Prepare and cook eggplants as in the recipe for *bonjon chalau* (p. 166). Prepare and cook short-grain rice as in the recipe for *bata* (p. 167).

SERVES **4**

SABZI BATA

Prepare and cook spinach as in the recipe for *sabzi chalau*, (p. 162). Prepare and cook short-grain rice as in the recipe for *bata* (p. 167). The dish can be eaten with a stew *(qorma)* if wished.

SERVES **4**

SHALGHAM BATA
Turnip Stew with Rice and Lamb

This tasty turnip stew is traditionally served with *bata* (see p. 167). It can also be served with *chalau* (p. 154).

⅔ cup vegetable oil
1 large onion, chopped
1½ lbs lamb on the bone
1 lb turnip, chopped into 1-inch cubes
2 tsp ground ginger
2 tsp ground cilantro
6 tbs brown sugar or molasses
salt and black pepper
1 lb (2 cups) white short-grain rice
¼ tsp saffron

Heat the oil in a pan and add the chopped onion. Fry over a medium to high heat until soft and golden brown. Add the meat and fry until the meat is golden brown and then add the chopped turnip and fry until brown. Add the ginger, ground cilantro, sugar and salt and pepper. Stir well and add ½ cup water. Bring to a boil, then turn down the heat and simmer until the meat is cooked and tender, adding more water to prevent sticking, if necessary. The sauce should be quite thick and not runny. The oil comes to the surface when the sauce is cooked.

Meanwhile wash the rice and put in a large pan with the 5 cups water. Add salt and bring to a boil, then turn down the heat and cook gently until the rice is soft and the water has evaporated. Add more water if necessary. Cover with a tightly fitting lid and put in a preheated oven at 300°F or cook over a low heat for half an hour. After half an hour, take the lid off and stir the rice. It should be thick and sticky. Spoon off ½ cup of oil from the surface of the stew. Add this oil to the rice and stir and mix again. Cover with the lid and cook for a further half an hour.

Before serving, add the saffron to the meat and turnips, stir well and leave on a low heat to blend for a minute or two.

Mound the rice onto a large dish, make a well in the center and fill with some of the juices from the meat and turnips. Put the rest in a separate dish.

SERVES 4

SHOLA GOSHTI

Sticky Rice with Meat

A recipe with many variations. This version was given to me by Abdul Ghaffour Redja. *Shola* is often made for *Nazer* (p. 11).

4 oz mung beans (or green lentils)
6 tbs vegetable oil
1 medium to large onion, finely chopped
8 oz boneless lamb or beef, in ¾-inch cubes
1 tbs tomato puree
3 cloves garlic, peeled and crushed
2 tsp powdered dill weed
salt and black pepper
8 oz (1 cup) short-grain rice
½ sweet bell pepper, chopped (optional)
1 tsp *char masala* (p. 27)

Wash the mung beans and soak for half an hour in warm water.

Heat 5 tablespoons of the oil in a pan and fry the chopped onions in it until reddish-brown. Add the meat, tomato puree and half of the crushed garlic. Stir well and continue frying until the meat becomes brown. Then add 2 cups water to the meat, followed by the mung beans, dill, salt and black pepper. Stir well and bring to a boil, then lower the heat, cover with a lid and cook gently for about 1 hour until the meat is tender. (If necessary add more water.)

While the meat is cooking, clean, wash and soak the rice.

When the meat is cooked, drain the rice and add it to the meat. Stir well, add the sweet pepper (if using), ½ cup water, cover with the lid, and turn the heat to low. Simmer the rice and meat slowly, stirring from time to time to prevent sticking, until the rice is soft and sticky and most of the water has been absorbed. Add more water if the rice becomes too dry. This takes about 30 minutes.

Fry the rest of the garlic in 1 tablespoon of oil until the color changes. Add to the meat and rice mixture. Stir in the *char masala*. Then place a thick clean cloth on top of the pan and cover with the lid. Leave the heat on low and cook slowly for another 30 minutes or so.

SERVES 3 TO 4

SHOLA-E-GHORBANDI
Sticky Rice with Mung Beans with a Plum Stew

Abdullah Afghanzada in his book *Local Dishes of Afghanistan* gives a little story of how this dish got its name. Ghorband is a beautiful and fertile area to the north of Kabul, renowned for its delicious fruits, especially grapes. One day a man from Kabul went to Ghorband to visit a friend unannounced. Afghan hospitality is legendary and the friend's wife on hearing about the unexpected guest and who was preparing only a simple and frugal dish of mung beans decided to add some rice to the cooking pot to make the meal go further. She had also cooked a little meat *qorma* separately. Instead of serving the rice and meat separately, she decided to make a hollow or well in the rice and add the *qorma* to it. The guest really enjoyed this tasty meal and on his return to Kabul told his wife all about it and asked her to reproduce the meal for him. And that is how this dish became known as *shola-e-Ghorbandi* (*shola* of Ghorband).

FOR THE *QORMA*:
2 oz yellow split peas
2 oz *olu bokhara* (see p. 38) or prunes
¼ cup vegetable oil
3 medium onions, finely chopped
1½ lbs lamb on the bone
1 tsp tomato puree
1 clove garlic, peeled and crushed
½ tsp turmeric
salt and red pepper

FOR THE *SHOLA*:
6 tbs vegetable oil
1 medium onion, finely chopped
1 clove garlic, peeled and crushed
3 oz split or ordinary mung beans
1 lb (2 cups) short-grain rice
1 tbs dill weed
salt and black pepper
1 - 2 tsp dried mint

First of all, soak the yellow split peas in warm water for about 2 hours. Also soak the *olu bokhara* in water. Set to one side.

Now prepare the *qorma*. Heat the vegetable oil in a pan and add the onions. Fry over a medium heat until soft and golden brown, then add the meat and continue frying until the meat has browned. Add the tomato puree, the crushed garlic and the turmeric. Fry for a couple of minutes more. Add enough water to just cover the meat and season with salt and red pepper to taste. Bring to a boil, then reduce the heat and boil gently until the meat is tender and the sauce thickened, about 1 hour or a little longer. Cook the split peas in plenty of water without salt until soft, then add to the *qorma* when the meat is tender.

Now prepare the *shola*. Heat the oil in a large pan and add the onions and crushed garlic. Fry until golden brown. Add the mung beans and stir until well coated in the oil. Add about 2¼ cups water to the mung beans, bring to a boil and then cook for about 15 to 20 minutes. Now add the rice, the dill and salt and plenty of black pepper. Add about another 2¼ cups water to cover the rice and mung beans by about 1¼ inches. Bring to a boil then cook gently until the rice and mung beans are cooked and the water has evaporated, adding more water if necessary. Now take about ½ cup of the juices from the *qorma* and mix into the rice and mung beans. Put the lid on the pan and place in the oven at a pre-heated temperature of 300°F for about half an hour.

When ready to serve, pile the rice up in a mound on a large platter, make a hollow or well in the center and then fill this with some of the *qorma*, serving the extra in a separate bowl. Sprinkle the whole dish with the mint.

SERVES 4

🐘 KETCHEREE QUROOT
Sticky Rice and Yogurt Dish

A very popular dish and distantly related to kedgeree, which evolved from *kichri*, a dish of rice and lentils. The *quroot* in its name is the dried yogurt described on p. 40; not easy to find or make, but the yogurt or *chaka* used in this recipe is a good substitute. This dish is served with *qorma* or *kofta*.

8 oz (1 cup) short-grain rice
2 oz mung beans (or green split peas)
6 tbs vegetable oil
salt
16 oz yogurt or *chaka* (p. 40)
2 cloves garlic, peeled and crushed
red pepper
2 tsp dried mint

Wash the rice and mung beans. Boil the latter in plenty of water until soft, then add the rice and enough water to cover by about 2 inches. Add the oil and 1 tsp of salt, stir, bring to a boil, cover with a lid, slightly ajar and cook gently over a medium low heat until the rice is soft and the water has evaporated (about ½ to 1 hour). Turn the heat to low and continue cooking for 20 to 30 minutes, stirring from time to time. The rice should have a thick, sticky consistency.

While the rice is cooking, prepare either meatballs in a sauce (follow the recipe for *kofta chalau* on p. 158, using 1 pound of minced meat and omitting the yogurt), or meat *qorma* (see the recipe for *qorma chalau* on p. 157).

Combine the yogurt with the garlic, a little salt, and a little red pepper.

When all is ready, mound the rice on a large dish and shape it with the back of a spoon. Make a well in the top and fill this with the yogurt, reserving some to serve separately. A little of the sauce from the meatballs or the *qorma* can be spooned over the rice. Finally, sprinkle with dried mint, and serve the meatballs or *qorma* separately.

SERVES 4

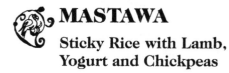

MASTAWA
Sticky Rice with Lamb, Yogurt and Chickpeas

Mastawa is a comforting dish for the winter months. It is traditionally made with dried meat called *gosht-e-qagh* (see p. 127). Dried meat like this is not readily available in the West, so this is an adapted version. The peel of Seville oranges gives a lovely, fragrant aroma and flavor to this dish. You can substitute ordinary orange peel if Seville oranges are not in season. I have used canned chickpeas for this recipe—I find them quicker and more convenient.

1½ lbs lamb on the bone, preferably shoulder of lamb
2 - 3 medium onions, finely sliced
½ tsp turmeric
1 medium/large orange, preferably Seville
1 lb (2 cups) short-grain rice
salt
16 oz yogurt (*chaka*, see p. 40)
3 - 4 cloves garlic, peeled and crushed
1 tbs vegetable oil
1 tbs powdered dill weed
½ - 1 tsp ground black pepper
1 can (14 oz) chickpeas, drained

Place the meat, cut into pieces, in a large pan with the onions. Add enough water to cover. Add the turmeric. Bring to a boil then cook gently until the meat is very tender and can easily be removed from the bones. This can take up to 1½ to 2 hours.

While the meat is cooking, cut the orange peel into thin matchstick-size strips, removing as much pith as possible. Leave to soak in a bowl of water.

When the meat is tender, remove from the pan and when cool enough remove the meat from the bones and shred the meat into strips with your hands. Return the meat to the pan. Wash the rice and then add to the pan with salt according to taste. The juices should cover the rice by about ¾ inch (add more water if necessary). Bring back to a boil, then reduce the heat to medium and cook with the lid off stirring from time to time until the rice is al dente and the liquid is absorbed. (You may need a little extra water).

Add the yogurt and stir in well but carefully.

Fry the crushed cloves of garlic in the oil and add to the meat and rice. Drain the orange peel and add this also to the dish along with the dill, black pepper, chickpeas and extra salt, to taste. Mix in well, then cover the top of the pan with a clean thick cloth and top with the lid. Leave on a low heat for about half an hour to allow the flavors to absorb. Then serve, perhaps with a salad.

SERVES 4

QORMA-E-OLU BOKHARA
Plum Stew

Olu bokhara (see p. 38) are small dried plums, which give a pleasant tart flavor to this dish. They are quite difficult to find for those without access to Persian shops. So it is useful to know that prunes can be substituted. Another variation is to use apricots (*zardolu*).

> 8 *olu bokhara* (or prunes or apricots)
> ½ cup vegetable oil
> 4 medium onions, finely chopped
> 2 lbs lamb on the bone, cut in chunks
> 1 tbs tomato puree
> 2 oz split peas
> 1 tsp cumin
> ½ tsp turmeric
> salt
> ½ tsp black pepper
> red pepper (optional)

Soak the *olu bokhara* or prunes in warm water (enough just to cover) for about half an hour.

Heat the oil in a pan and add the chopped onions. Fry over a medium to high heat, stirring frequently until golden brown and soft. Add the lamb and fry again until the meat and onions are well browned. Mix in the tomato puree and continue frying for a minute or two. Add split peas, the spices, salt and black and red pepper (if using) and enough water to just cover. Bring to a boil, then turn the heat down and simmer until the meat and split peas are just about cooked, about 1 to 1¼ hours. Add the *olu bokhara* or prunes with the water in which they were soaked, then simmer for another 20 to 30 minutes until the sauce has thickened and the flavors have blended.

Serve with *chalau*.

SERVES 4

QORMA-E-KASHMIRI
Lamb or Chicken Stew with Yogurt

Zobeida Sekanderi, who gave me this recipe, told me that it originally came from Kashmir, as the name implies. Lamb can be substituted for the chicken if preferred.

3 large onions, finely chopped
¼ cup vegetable oil
1 medium/large chicken, jointed
2 - 3 cloves garlic, minced
½ - 1 tsp turmeric
salt and black pepper
½ - 1 tsp aniseed
8 oz yogurt (*chaka*, see p. 40)
handful fresh chopped mint or 1 tbs dried mint
1 tbs tomato puree (optional)

Fry the onions gently in the oil until soft and transparent. Add the chicken to the onions and fry until golden brown. Add the garlic, turmeric, salt and black pepper. Stir and fry for about 2 minutes. Add the aniseed. Add about 6 tablespoons water and then cook gently until the chicken is cooked and tender, about 40 minutes.

When the chicken is almost ready, reduce the heat and stir in the yogurt slowly, stirring all the time. Then turn up the heat to medium and cook for a little longer, until the sauce has thickened and the flavors blend (15 to 30 minutes). Just before serving add the mint. (Do not add the mint too early as the taste of the mint will go bitter.) Add the tomato puree, if used. Stir well and serve with *chalau*.

SERVES 4

☙ QORMA-E-KAUK
Partridge Stew

Game birds in Afghanistan included the partridge, called *kauk*. Louis Dupree in his book *Afghanistan*, says that the "chukar" partridge is the red-billed, red-legged species, about the size of a small chicken; and that apart from being enjoyed as food it was used for fighting.

I remember seeing in the bazaars what he calls the "sisi" partridge. This is much smaller, and more like a quail, which is called a *bod bada* in Dari. Dupree also describes the francolin (black partridge). I have found that quail, often more readily available than partridge, is a good substitute.

2 oz yellow split peas
3 medium onions, finely chopped
¼ cup vegetable oil
4 *kauk* (quail or small partridge)
1 tbs tomato paste
2 whole green cardamom pods
salt and pepper
4 - 6 *olu bokhara* (see p. 38) or prunes, soaked (optional)

First of all cook the split peas in plenty of boiling water, skimming off any froth as and when necessary, until just soft.

Fry the onions in the oil until golden brown, then add the *kauk*. (In Afghanistan as the *kauk* tended to be a little tough, they would first of all be steamed a little before cooking). Fry until the *kauk* are golden brown, then stir in the tomato paste, fry for a minute or two, then add enough water to just cover. Add the cardamom, salt and pepper and the split peas and cook slowly for about half an hour or so, until the *kauk* are nicely tender. The *olu bokhara*, if used, should be added in the last few minutes of cooking and the flavors allowed to blend.

Serve with *chalau*, a salad and perhaps some chutney or pickles.

SERVES 4

꒜ QORMA-E-GUL-E-KARAM
Cauliflower Stew

Cauliflower is a popular vegetable in the winter months in Afghanistan and many families prepared it with meat as in this recipe. However, it can be just as easily be prepared without meat, making it suitable for vegetarians. Mahwash Amani gave me this recipe. It is best served with *chalau* or with *nan*.

2 medium onions, finely chopped
¼ cup vegetable oil
1 lb lamb or beef, cut into 1-inch cubes
1½ tsp split yellow peas
1 tbs tomato puree or 2 tsp ground cilantro seed
salt and pepper to taste
1 clove of garlic, peeled and chopped or crushed
½ tsp turmeric
1 large cauliflower

Fry the onions gently in the oil until golden brown and soft. Then add the meat. Fry and stir well for a few minutes until the meat is browned, then add split peas and the tomato puree or cilantro. Stir well for a couple of minutes then add the salt, pepper, garlic and turmeric. Add enough water to just cover the meat. Boil gently until the meat is nearly cooked, then add the cauliflower. Cook gently until the cauliflower and split peas are soft and the sauce is quite thick.

SERVES 4

✿ QORMA-E-ZARDAK
Carrot Stew

My sister-in-law Najiba Zaka, who gave me this recipe, likes most of all to serve this stew with *mantu* (see p. 87), but it can also accompany a *pilau* or *chalau*. If served with *chalau* it is then called *zardak chalau*. It is also delicious just eaten with fresh *nan*. This dish can also be made with the addition of meat, if desired. In that case omit the split peas, vinegar and sugar and add the meat, cut into cubes, when the onions are golden brown. Also, do not add the carrots until the meat is almost cooked.

    8 oz split yellow peas
    2 medium onions, peeled and finely chopped
    ¼ cup vegetable oil
    1 lb carrots, peeled and diced
    2 tomatoes
    1 tsp turmeric
    1 clove garlic, peeled and crushed
    ¼ cup sugar
    salt and black pepper
    1 tsp vinegar

Soak the split peas in a little warm water for about half an hour or so before cooking.

Fry the chopped onion gently in the oil until golden brown and soft. Drain the peas and add to the onion. Now add enough water to cover and bring to a boil. Add all the other ingredients, adjusting sugar to taste. Stir well and cook slowly, stirring from time to time, until all the carrots and split peas are cooked, adding extra water if the stew becomes too dry.

SERVES **4**

QORMA-E-SAIB

Apple Stew

This is a slightly sweet *qorma* well liked by Afghans. It is spiced with the addition of ginger and chilies and the meat can be boneless, if preferred.

6 tbs vegetable oil
3 medium onions, finely chopped
2 lbs lamb on the bone or chicken, cut into chunks
4 apples
6 tbs sugar
1 tsp ground ginger
½ tsp red pepper
½ tsp ground green cardamom
salt
2 tsp lemon juice

Heat 4 tablespoons of the oil in a pan and add the onions. Fry over a medium/high heat until soft and golden brown. Now add the meat and fry well until browning. Add about a cup of water (just enough to cover the meat) mix well and cook gently until the meat is tender.

When the meat is almost cooked, peel and core the apples and cut each into eight pieces. Fry them gently in the remaining 2 tablespoons of oil for a couple of minutes. Sprinkle the sugar over the apples and then add them to the *qorma*. Season with the ginger, red pepper, cardamom and salt to taste. Sprinkle in the lemon juice. Cook gently for a further 10 minutes until the apples and meat are soft and the oil has separated out.

SERVES **4**

QORMA-E-BEHI
Quince Stew

The flavor of this stew is slightly sweet but is spiced up by the ginger, cardamom and chilies. The lamb can be on the bone or boneless. Adjust quantities accordingly.

2 large quinces
6 tbs vegetable oil
3 medium onions, preferably red, finely chopped
2 lbs lamb on the bone, cut into chunks
1 tsp ground ginger
½ tsp cayenne pepper
½ tsp ground cardamom
½ cup brown sugar or molasses
salt

Peel the quinces and cut into 1-inch cubes.

Heat the oil in a pan and then add the finely chopped onions. Fry over a medium/high heat until soft and golden brown. Now add the meat and fry until browning, then add the quince. Stir, then add the spices. Fry for about a minute then add about a cup of water, to just cover the meat and quince, the sugar and salt to taste. Stir the ingredients and cook gently until the meat is tender and quinces are soft, about 45 minutes to 1 hour.

Serve with *chalau*.

SERVES 4

🦚 QORMA-E-SAMARUQ
Mushroom Stew

The mushrooms in Afghanistan are, I believe, sulphur shelf mushrooms, which are very "meaty." For this recipe I suggest that large, stuffing mushrooms could be used as they are of similar texture.

1 medium/large onion, finely chopped
6 tbs vegetable oil
1 lb boneless chicken or lamb, cut into serving-size portions
1 can (14 oz) chopped tomatoes
¼ tsp red pepper or 1 green chili
¼ tsp turmeric
¼ tsp ground fennel seeds
¼ tsp ground ginger
salt
12 oz mushrooms, roughly chopped

Fry the onions in the oil until golden brown. Now add the chicken or lamb and fry further until browning, then add the chopped tomatoes, spices and salt, to taste. Fry until the meat is almost cooked, then add the mushrooms. Cook gently to allow the flavors to develop and the mushrooms to cook, about 15 to 20 minutes.

Serve with a *chalau* and perhaps some fresh *nan*.

SERVES 4

❦ QORMA-E-RAWASH
Rhubarb Stew

Rhubarb is considered a "cold" food and is used medicinally as it is considered good for cleansing the blood and purifying the system.

> 3 medium onions, finely chopped
> 6 tbs vegetable oil
> 1½ lbs boneless lamb, cut into 1-inch cubes
> 1 tbs tomato puree
> 1 tsp *char masala* (see p. 27) or ground cilantro
> salt and black pepper
> 1 lb rhubarb
> small bunch fresh cilantro or mint,
>   finely chopped

Fry the onions in the vegetable oil over a medium heat until soft and golden brown. Add the meat and continue frying until brown. Stir in the tomato puree and fry for a minute or two. Add about ½ cup water, the *char masala* and salt and pepper and bring to a boil. Turn down the heat and simmer until the meat is cooked.

Meanwhile wash the rhubarb and cut into 2-inch lengths. Boil in a small amount of water until it is soft, but not disintegrating.

Just before serving drain the rhubarb and place over the top of the *qorma*. Garnish with the fresh cilantro.

Serve with *chalau*.

SERVES 4

Tabang wala.

Vegetable Dishes and Salads

Whenever I was in Afghanistan, the bazaars were full of cheap, good quality vegetables in season. Common vegetables include cauliflower, carrots, cabbage, turnips, marrows, pumpkins, spinach, potatoes, peas, lady's fingers (okra), leeks and French beans. These vegetables are usually added to a meat stew *(qorma)* and eaten with rice or *nan*. (If meat is not available, a vegetable *qorma* is made.) Some vegetables, such as potatoes, corn on the cob and eggplants, are placed in the dying embers of the *tandoor* and cooked overnight, to be eaten for breakfast the next morning. When potatoes are cooked in this fashion they were called *katchalu-e-khorayi*.

Onions are essential for many dishes. They are used in soups *(sherwa)*, stews *(qorma)* and often in *pilaus*. They are also eaten raw in salads. *Gandana* is another important vegetable (p. 34).

Tomatoes in season are plentiful and cheap. They are used to add color and flavor to dishes, eaten raw in salads or just on their own with a little salt. Afghans make chutneys and puree from the abundant tomatoes in summer for use during the winter months. Tomatoes, and also other vegetables such as chilies, eggplants and onions are often dried. Eggplants and sweet peppers are cooked in several ways, and are essential for some special vegetable dishes such as *burani bonjon* and *dolma*.

Raw vegetables such as radishes, scallions, cucumbers and lettuce are mainly eaten in salads or side dishes but are sometimes served as a quick snack with *nan*. A typical Afghan salad includes all these ingredients as well as tomatoes, and perhaps sweet peppers. There are no really hard and fast rules about how to prepare salads in Afghanistan, except that they are nearly always sprinkled with salt and lemon or *norinj* (bitter orange) juice and left to marinate for about half an hour before serving. Vinegar is rarely used, and only very occasionally is olive or other oil added. Fresh cilantro is often added to salads, either chopped finely or left whole for garnishing. Mint is another herb often used to flavor or garnish salads. Sometimes hot green or red chilies are added either whole or finely chopped (with seeds removed).

Pulses are important in the Afghan diet as they often replace meat (see p. 33). Red kidney beans, chickpeas, and split peas are the most common and are usually added to stews or soups. Mung beans are added to rice dishes such as *shola*.

DOLMA MURCH-E-SHIREEN
Stuffed Bell Peppers

This dish invites variations. The filling suggested can also be used to stuff tomatoes and eggplants, cabbage and vine leaves; the cooking time will vary, but it is always quick and simple to make and can be a meal in itself. If something more substantial is required it can be served with *chalau* or *pilau*.

4 oz (10 tbs) short- or long-grain rice
4 large green or red bell peppers
6 tbs vegetable oil
1 lb minced beef or lamb
2 medium onions, finely chopped
1 tsp ground cilantro
salt and pepper

Wash the rice and soak it in clean water for 30 minutes.

Prepare the peppers by cutting off the stems end and scooping out the seeds.

Heat 4 tablespoons of the oil in a pan and fry the meat and onions until they are brown. Turn down the heat and simmer for 10 to 15 minutes. Drain the rice and add to the meat mixture, then add the cilantro, salt and pepper, and mix well. Fill the peppers with the meat mixture and fasten the tops of the peppers in place with toothpicks.

Place the prepared *dolma* in a deep pan. Add water so that it comes a third of the way up the *dolma*. Add the remaining 2 tablespoons of oil and salt and pepper to taste. Bring to a boil, then reduce the heat and continue to boil gently. Turn the *dolma* occasionally to ensure that they are evenly cooked. The cooking time is 30 to 45 minutes.

Serve on a warm dish with some of the juices spooned over.

SERVES 4

DOLMA BARG-E-KARAM
Stuffed Cabbage Leaves

This can also be made with vine leaves. Cooking time will vary according to the freshness of the leaves.

    4 oz (10 tbs) short- or long-grain rice
    8 - 12 cabbage leaves (or vine leaves)
    6 tbs vegetable oil
    1 lb minced beef or lamb
    2 medium onions, finely chopped
    1 tsp ground cilantro
    salt and pepper

Wash the rice and soak it in clean water for about 30 minutes.

Prepare the meat filling as in the recipe for *dolma murch-e-shireen* on the preceding page.

Remove the leaves from the head of a cabbage; the number you require depends on the size of the leaves. Drop the leaves into boiling salted water and boil for a couple of minutes. (If the main rib is too thick, cut it out.)

Put an amount of cooked filling appropriate to its size on each leaf. Form into sausage shapes by rolling up the leaves tightly and tucking in the ends. Lay the *dolma* in a single layer on the bottom of a pan. Add enough water or stock to cover, add the remaining 2 tablespoons of oil, salt and pepper and cook gently, covered, for 25 to 30 minutes.

This dish improves with standing and can be cooked in advance and then reheated. Serve on a warmed dish with a little of the juice spooned over the top.

SERVES 4

BURANI BONJON
Eggplant with Yogurt

Buran is the name given to a vast range of dishes extending from Spain to the Balkans as well as the Islamic heartland extending from Morocco to India. Its history is long and complicated and the legend behind the dish has many versions. According to Charles Perry in his article in *The Oxford Companion to Food,* Buran was the nickname of the princess who married the caliph of Baghdad in the ninth century and *buran* has evolved from the special dish served at her lavish wedding celebration.

In Afghanistan this dish is known as *burani* and it has evolved into a wide range of vegetable dishes served with a yogurt-based sauce.

Everyone loves this dish, it is really so delicious. But I have been mildly rebuked and criticized by friends about the recipe I gave in the first edition of this book. They all say that the amounts I give are just not enough. So I make amends here and hope that I have finally got it right! My family enjoys the dish on its own with freshly baked *nan*, but it is equally good with a *chalau* or *pilau*.

2 - 3 large eggplants
vegetable oil for frying
1 medium onion, finely chopped
1 - 2 medium tomatoes, thinly sliced
1 green bell pepper, finely sliced in rings (optional)
¼ - ½ tsp red pepper
salt
16 oz strained yogurt (*chaka* p. 40)
2 cloves garlic, peeled and crushed
2 tsp dried mint

Peel the eggplants and slice them into rounds about ¼ - ½ inch thick.

Heat plenty of vegetable oil in a frying pan (eggplants soak up a lot of oil) and fry as many slices of the eggplant as possible in one layer. Fry on both sides until brown. Remove from the pan and drain on absorbent paper towels. Repeat with the remaining slices, adding more oil as necessary.

Fry the chopped onions in a little oil until reddish-brown. Slice the tomatoes. Arrange the eggplants, tomatoes, sliced pepper and onions in layers in a pan, sprinkling each layer with a little salt and a little red pepper. Add 2 to 3 tablespoons of water, cover the pan with a lid and simmer over a low heat for about 30 minutes.

Meanwhile combine the strained yogurt, the crushed garlic, a little salt and the dried mint.

Put half of the yogurt on to a warm serving dish. Carefully remove the eggplants from the pan with a spatula, and arrange them on the yogurt. Dot the rest of the yogurt on top and sprinkle on any remaining sauce (but not the oil) from the eggplants. Serve immediately.

SERVES 4

NOTE:
Some people have told me that for a more healthful dish they brush the eggplant slices with oil and brown them under the broiler. It uses less oil, but I still prefer frying them.

BURANI KADU
Squash with Yogurt

This recipe, which was given to me by Valerie Hachimzai, is a less rich alternative to *burani bonjon*.

1 large summer squash (about 1½ lbs)
¼ cup vegetable oil
1 large onion, chopped
1 medium/large tomato, sliced
salt
red pepper
16 oz strained yogurt (*chaka* p. 40)

Peel the squash and cut into 1-inch rings. Scoop out the seeds. (The squash can also be cut into 1-inch cubes if preferred.)

Heat the oil in a large pan which has a lid, and fry the onion in it over a medium heat until soft and golden brown. Add the squash, fry it on both sides for a couple of minutes, and mix in the tomatoes, salt, and pepper. Cover, turn the heat to low and cook for 30 to 40 minutes, or until the squash is cooked and most of the liquid has evaporated. (Water will have come out of the squash and tomato, so it is not necessary to add any to this dish.)

To serve, put half of the yogurt on to a warmed dish and arrange the squash on this. Top with the remaining yogurt and any leftover cooking juices. Serve immediately; suitable accompaniments are a rice dish or plain *nan*.

SERVES 4

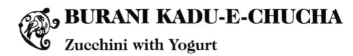

BURANI KADU-E-CHUCHA
Zucchini with Yogurt

We were not able to get zucchini when I lived in Afghanistan, only squash, so I have called this *burani* "baby squash" as *chucha* means "baby." This recipe is a version of *burani* adapted by Afghans living in exile in the West. I first tasted it at Rahila Reshnou's house and she showed me how to make it. I like to serve it with *yahkoot pilau* (see p. 139), although it is equally delicious with *chalau* or as a snack with *nan*.

4 - 6 medium zucchini
2 tbs vegetable oil
½ green bell pepper, sliced (optional)
1 green chili, chopped finely (optional)
1 tbs tomato puree
1 tsp ground cilantro
salt and pepper
2 cloves garlic, peeled and crushed
2 tsp dried mint
red pepper (optional)
16 oz strained yogurt (*chaka* p. 40)

Slice the zucchini about ½-inch thick. Heat the oil in a pan, and add the zucchini. Fry gently in the oil, coating on all sides. Add the green pepper and chili if desired. Continue frying gently until the zucchini are a golden brown. Now add the tomato puree and about a tablespoon of water. Mix gently, then add the cilantro, and salt and pepper to taste.

Cover with a lid and simmer slowly until the zucchini are tender. This does not take long (10 to 15 minutes).

Meanwhile, add salt, the crushed garlic, mint, and a pinch or two of red pepper, if desired, to the yogurt. Stir and mix.

When the zucchini are ready, spoon about half of the yogurt onto a warm serving dish, add the zucchini and their juices on top, then dot the remaining yogurt mixture over all.

SERVES 4

BURANI KATCHALU
Potatoes with Yogurt

This is another *burani* recipe that my sister-in-law Najiba taught me. It makes a tasty midday snack. Enjoy it with freshly baked *nan*.

4 - 6 medium to large potatoes
4 tbs cooking oil
1 medium to large onion, finely chopped
1 tbs tomato puree
1 tbs finely chopped fresh cilantro
½ tsp turmeric
salt and black pepper
2 cloves garlic, peeled
16 oz strained yogurt (*chaka* p. 40)
red pepper

Peel and wash the potatoes. Cut into chunks or slices about ½-inch thick. Set to one side. Heat the oil, add the onions and fry gently in oil until golden brown. Next add the tomato puree and cook for a further 1 to 2 minutes until brown. Add about ½ cup water and the chopped cilantro. Bring to a boil, then simmer until the sauce has thickened a little. Add the potatoes, turmeric, and salt and black pepper. Now stir carefully until the potatoes are coated with the sauce, adding more water if necessary (the sauce should remain thick, not watery). Cook gently on a low heat, stirring carefully from time to time so as not to break up the potatoes too much. Again add more water if the sauce is becoming too dry. This will very much depend on the type of potatoes you use. Cook until the potatoes are cooked through and soft, but not mushy.

While the potatoes are cooking, crush or finely chop the garlic and add to the yogurt. Add a little salt and a little red pepper to taste.

Spoon and spread about half of the yogurt over a warm serving dish then arrange the potatoes on top. Add spoonfuls of the remaining yoghurt on top and serve any extra in a separate bowl. Serve with freshly baked *nan*.

SERVES **4**

LAWANG-E-SAMARUQ
Mushrooms in Yogurt

It is best to use the large stuffing mushrooms, which have a meatier taste, for this dish. However ordinary field mushrooms can be substituted.

2 medium onions, peeled and finely chopped
¼ cup vegetable oil
1 clove garlic, peeled and finely chopped
1 lb (450 g) mushrooms, cut into 1-inch cubes
1 green chili
½ tsp turmeric
salt
½ cup strained yogurt (*chaka* p. 40)

Fry the onions in the oil until soft and golden brown. Add the garlic, mushrooms, chili, turmeric and salt and fry together until the mushrooms are nicely browned. Add just under 1 cup water and simmer until the mushrooms are cooked. Now add the yogurt and heat through for about 5 minutes.
Serve with *chalau*.

SERVES 4

SABZI RAHWASH
Spinach with Rhubarb

Afghans often cook rhubarb and spinach together, an unusual and tasty vegetable dish, which can be served with *chalau* or *pilau,* or with a *qorma* and fresh *nan.*

2 lbs spinach
8 oz leeks, scallions or *gandana* (p. 34)
6 tbs vegetable oil
2 tbs powdered dill weed
salt and pepper
2 oz rhubarb

Wash the spinach thoroughly, remove the stems and roughly chop. Wash the leeks well and chop into small pieces.

Heat 4 tablespoons of vegetable oil in a pan and fry the chopped leeks over a medium to high heat. When they are soft but not brown, add the spinach and stir continuously until the spinach reduces. Reduce the heat, cover, and continue to cook gently, stirring occasionally, until the oil comes to the surface, about 15 or 20 minutes. Then add the dill, salt and pepper. Add a little water if necessary.

While the spinach is cooking, skin and wash the rhubarb and cut it into 1-inch lengths. Fry it briefly in the remaining 2 table-spoons of oil over a medium heat, without letting it brown, then add it to the spinach and cook for a further half an hour or until it is soft.

SERVES 4

BOMYA or QORMA-E-SHAST-E-ARUS

Okra Stew

Shast-e-arus in Dari means "bride's finger." Okra is sometimes called lady fingers.

1 lb okra (use young, small ones)
6 tbs vegetable oil
1 medium onion, chopped
1 oz split peas
1 can (7 oz) tomatoes
salt and pepper
1 tsp powdered dill weed

Clean the okra and cut off the stalks.

Heat the oil in a pan and fry the chopped onion until brown. Add the okra and fry gently, stirring carefully until they are well coated with the oil. Add the split peas, tomatoes, salt and pepper, stir the ingredients, and then cook over a medium heat for a few minutes. Next, add water to just cover the okra, and add the dill. Bring back to a boil, then turn down the heat and simmer for 30 to 45 minutes or until the liquid has reduced, the sauce has thickened, and the oil has come to the surface.

This *qorma* is usually served with *chalau*, although it can be served with a *pilau*.

SERVES 4

DAL
A Lentil Dish

Dal is an economical dish, similar to the Indian dish of the same name, and eaten with *chalau* or *yakhni pilau*. Sometimes minced meat is served with the rice and *dal,* but never a meat *qorma.*

8 oz *moong dal* (p. 34)
1 medium onion, chopped
1 - 2 cloves garlic, peeled and crushed
3 tbs vegetable oil
½ tsp ground ginger
½ tsp turmeric
1 - 2 tsp tomato puree
salt and pepper

Wash the *dal* in cold water, drain, and then put into a pan with enough water to cover it by about 2 inches. Bring to a boil. Remove any surface scum, then cover (but leave the lid slightly ajar), turn the heat to low and simmer for about half an hour. Stir often to prevent sticking.

Fry the chopped onion and half of the crushed garlic in 2 tablespoons of the oil until lightly browned. Add the ginger, turmeric and tomato puree. Stir and fry for a minute or two. Now add these ingredients to the *dal,* together with more water so that the level is 1 inch above the *dal.* Season with salt and pepper, and simmer until the water has evaporated and the *dal* is well cooked; thick but runny. This takes about an hour.

Just before serving fry the remaining garlic in the remaining 1 tablespoon of oil and pour over the *dal.*

SERVES 4

SALATA
Mixed Salad

Salad is usually prepared as a "*maza*," i.e. something tasty to eat before the main meal is served or as a side dish to go with rice dishes or kebabs. As mentioned in the introduction to this section, there are no really hard and fast rules about making a salad in Afghanistan. Afghans use whatever is fresh and in season. This is a salad I frequently make at home. I often add a little chopped celery, which gives a lovely flavor, although I hasten to add that this was not a vegetable we used in Afghanistan.

  1 small/medium cos or romaine lettuce
  4 scallions
  4 red or pink radishes
  3 - 4 tomatoes
  ½ green or red bell pepper
  1 hot green chili (optional)
  ¼ cucumber
  2 tbs fresh cilantro or mint
  salt
  juice of ½ - 1 lemon

Wash all of the ingredients (except the lemon), topping and tailing the scallions and radishes first. Shred the lettuce into long strips. Chop the scallions, radishes and tomatoes into small pieces or dice. Cut the bell pepper in half and remove the seeds, then finely chop. Repeat with the hot green chili. Peel the cucumber and also dice. Finely chop the fresh cilantro or mint.

Place all these prepared ingredients in a salad bowl. Sprinkle liberally with salt and then sprinkle with the lemon juice. Toss well, but carefully, to mix all the ingredients.

SERVES 4

 **SALATA II**

This is more like a relish than a salad. I particularly remember that Abdul Majid, the cook who worked for me at the British Embassy in Kabul, used to like making this salad to go with rice dishes or kebabs. Abdul and his friend Hamidullah, often came to help me with big parties after I had married. I really miss Abdul's cool and professional manner in the kitchen and Hamidullah's smiling face as he used to help serve the drinks. The secret of this salad is that it should be very finely chopped and the chili adds a bit of extra kick.

4 tomatoes
½ cucumber
½ onion
1 hot green chili, seeds removed
1 small bunch fresh cilantro, washed
juice of ½ lemon
salt

Finely chop all the ingredients. Place in a bowl. Sprinkle with the lemon juice and salt and mix well.

SALATA BONJON-E-RUMI-WA-PIAZ
Tomato and Onion Salad

This is often prepared as a side dish to go with rice dishes or kebabs. It is also eaten as a snack with fresh *nan*. Some Afghans add hot green chilies and finely chop all the ingredients.

    1 medium onion, finely sliced
    salt
    1 - 2 cloves garlic, peeled and crushed
    juice of half a lemon
    4 medium/large tomatoes, thinly sliced
    3 tbs finely chopped fresh cilantro leaves (reserve a few sprigs
       for garnishing)

Place the finely sliced onions in a bowl and add about 1 teaspoon of salt. Mix well, then rinse in water and drain.

Add the crushed garlic and a little salt to the lemon juice.

Mix the sliced tomatoes and onions together with the finely chopped cilantro. Add the lemon juice and garlic and leave to marinate in a cool place for about 30 minutes.

Serve on a flat dish or in a bowl, garnished with sprigs of cilantro.

SERVES **4**

Pickles
and
Chutneys

Pickles and chutneys, *turshi* and *chutni,* are an essential part of Afghan food. Rarely is a meal served without one home-made speciality. When various fruits and vegetables are in season, plentiful and cheap, there is a flurry of activity in making pickles and chutney to be stored for the times when fresh vegetables and fruits are scarce.

Turshi, (*tursh* means "sour") are made from a variety of vegetables including baby eggplants, carrots, beans, chilies, small onions, limes or lemons and squash. Chutneys include peach or apricot and cilantro, mint and red pepper.

Many Afghans living in the West have told me that they use malt vinegar for making chutneys and pickles. But I know that vinegar is also made from grapes, which are abundant in Afghanistan. The choice is yours but quantities may have to be adjusted according to taste.

 TURSHI LIMO
Lemon Pickle

There are many recipes for the traditional lemon pickle, of which I give two. It is usually made with the very small lemons or limes which are readily available in Afghanistan, but ordinary lemons can be used in the first recipe.

1 lb lemons or limes
½ tbs *sia dona* (nigella seeds)
½ tbs fenugreek
½ tbs sugar
1 tbs salt

Cut the lemons in half, squeeze out and reserve the juice. Scoop out the insides and, if the lemons are large, cut the halves into two. Put them into salted water for 24 hours.

Take the lemon peels from the water and boil as many times as necessary in fresh, clean water to remove all bitterness and make them soft. Drain, then boil them again, this time in the lemon juice, for a couple of minutes. Add the rest of the ingredients, leave to cool, then place in clean, dry jars and screw on lids ready to store. The lemon peels should always be covered by lemon juice in the jars, so add extra lemon juice if required.

MAKES ABOUT 2 ONE-POUND JARS

TURSHI LIMO II

2 lbs very small lemons or limes
1 tbs *sia dona* (nigella seeds)
1 tbs fenugreek
1 tbs sugar
2 tbs salt

Squeeze out the juice from half of the lemons and reserve. Puncture holes in the skins of the remaining lemons before putting inside clean, dry jars. Add the lemon juice and the other ingredients. If the lemons are not covered by juice, add more lemon juice and proportionately more sugar. Screw on the lids and leave in a warm and preferably sunny place until the lemons become soft and are no longer bitter. How long this takes depends upon where the jars are placed. If the juice evaporates, add more lemon juice.

MAKES ABOUT 4 ONE-POUND JARS

TURSHI ZARDAK

Carrot Pickle

This pickle can also be made with canned carrots. The taste of the vinegar may be too strong for some people; it can be diluted by using a little water or liquid from the can of carrots.

1 hot green chili
7 oz small, young carrots or a small 7-oz can
vinegar
½ tsp salt
½ tsp *sia dona* (nigella seeds)
1 clove garlic, peeled and crushed
2 tsp sugar

Boil the hot green chili in a little water for about 5 minutes until soft, then chop it into small pieces.

Scrape, dice and wash the carrots. (If using a can drain off the liquid.) Put the carrots in a pan and add just enough vinegar to cover them. Boil for about 3 minutes. Add the salt, *sia dona*, crushed garlic, sugar and the hot green chili. Mix well and put into a clean, dry jar, adding more vinegar if necessary in order to cover the carrots. Screw on the lid and leave for a few days.

MAKES ABOUT 1 ONE-POUND JAR

TURSHI TARKARI
Mixed Vegetable Pickle

I first tasted this excellent pickle at Mahwash Amani's house and she kindly gave me the recipe. The amount of vinegar may be too strong for some tastes, so can be diluted with a little water if preferred. Likewise, the amount of garlic and chilies can be increased or decreased, although it is really these flavors which give this pickle its distinctly sharp and delicious taste. It goes particularly well with savory rice dishes.

1 medium eggplant
8 oz carrots
8 oz white savoy cabbage
1 small cauliflower
20 oz (2½ cups) white or red wine vinegar
4 - 6 hot green chilies
4 - 8 cloves garlic, peeled
2 tbs salt
1 tbs mint or dill

Peel the eggplants and dice into ½-inch cubes. Scrape, dice and wash the carrots. Remove the outer leaves of the cabbage and chop into thick slices in one direction and then thickly in the other direction. Leave in chunks. Wash and drain. Separate the cauliflower into small florets and then wash and drain.

Place all the prepared vegetables in a pan and pour the vinegar over them. Bring to a boil, then simmer for about 5 minutes. Remove from the heat.

Meanwhile finely chop up the hot green chilies, removing the seeds first and then crush the garlic. Add the chilies, the crushed garlic, salt and mint to the poached vegetables. Mix well and when cool enough place the vegetable and vinegar mixture into clean jars. Make sure that the vegetables are well covered with vinegar, adding more if necessary. Seal the jars and leave for 2 or 3 days in a refrigerator or cool place.

MAKES ABOUT 4 TO 5 ONE-POUND JARS

TURSHI BONJON-E-SIA
Eggplant Pickle

My favorite pickle; it is best made with "baby"eggplants, if you can find them. If not you can substitute ordinary eggplants cut into ½-inch cubes.

1 lb baby eggplants
10 - 20 garlic cloves, peeled
1 heaped tsp turmeric
2 - 3 oz fresh green chilies
1 tbs *sia dona* (nigella seed)
1 tbs fenugreek seeds
1 tsp salt
½ tbs dried mint
½ tsp sugar
18 oz (2¼ cups) vinegar
10 tbs boiled water

Slit the eggplants lengthwise to the stalk, but do not separate. Put one clove of garlic inside each split eggplant.

Bring a pan of water to a boil and add the turmeric. Add the eggplants. The water should cover the eggplants well and you will have to press them down into the boiling water from time to time as they will bob up to the surface. Turn down the heat and boil gently for about 5 minutes or until the eggplants are just cooked. Remove from the water with a slotted spoon and drain. Next, place the eggplants in a large jar or jars by putting a layer of eggplants, then a layer of chilies and continue in this way until they are all used up. Now mix the *sia dona*, fenugreek, salt, mint and sugar to the vinegar, followed by the boiled water, mix well and pour over the vegetables in the jars. The ingredients should be well covered with the liquid; if not, top with more vinegar. Cover and seal with a lid. Leave for several days in a refrigerator or cool place.

MAKES ABOUT 4 ONE-POUND JARS

CHUTNI BONJON-E-RUMI
Tomato Chutney

My sister-in-law used to make large amounts of tomato chutney when tomatoes were cheap and plentiful in the summer months in Kabul.

8 oz white onions
1 - 2 hot red chilies
1 lb tomatoes
2 cloves garlic, peeled and crushed
3 tbs vinegar
1 - 2 tsp salt
2 tsp sugar
1 tsp *sia dona* (nigella seeds)

Peel the onions and then either grate them or chop into small pieces in a blender. Reserve. Cut up the tomatoes roughly and puree them in a blender with the red chilies or push through a wire mesh. Now mix the tomatoes, chilies, onions and garlic together and add the vinegar, salt, sugar and *sia dona*. Mix well, then store in clean dry jars in a cool place.

This is served like cilantro chutney and goes well with kebabs and *pakaura*.

MAKES ABOUT 2 ONE-POUND JARS

CHUTNI OLU BOLU

Sour Cherry Chutney

I was given this recipe by an Afghan friend. She told me that it goes very well with kebabs. She also advised that the walnuts should be as fresh as possible, since dark, rancid walnuts will spoil the flavor. Sour cherries are not always easy to find, so I have also tried making this chutney with sweet, dark red cherries with red flesh. It works quite well, but of course, the color and flavor are not quite the same. The taste of ordinary cherries is sweeter so to counteract this I suggest increasing the amount of vinegar.

1 lb sour cherries
2 hot green chilies, finely chopped
3 cloves garlic, peeled and crushed
3 tbs finely chopped walnuts
1 tsp salt
1 tsp - 1 tbs vinegar

Wash the cherries and dry them. Discard the stones and roughly chop the cherries. Put in a blender with the chilies, garlic and walnuts and mix until a paste is formed (about the consistency of tomato puree). Do not blend too much. Add salt according to taste and the vinegar. Sometimes, instead of vinegar, a little yogurt is mixed in with the chutney for a change.

MAKES ABOUT 2 ONE-POUND JARS

CHUTNI SHAFTOLU/ZARD OLU

Peach or Apricot Chutney

This recipe has been adapted so that canned peaches or apricots may be used.

    1 can (1 lb 13 oz) peaches or apricots
    1 - 2 hot green chilies, seeds removed, finely chopped
    9 oz (1 cup plus 2 tbs) white wine vinegar
    1 tsp *sia dona* (nigella seeds)
    1 tbs ground ginger
    1 tbs salt

Drain the peaches reserving the syrup if you wish to add it later. Mash them with a fork, and combine with the green chilies. Boil the vinegar for 5 minutes, then add to it the *sia dona*, ginger, salt and (if wished) a little of the syrup from the peaches. Remove the vinegar from the heat and add the peaches and chilies. When cool, place in clean dry jars with tightly fitting lids. Store in a cool place or in a refrigerator.

MAKES 2 ONE-POUND JARS

CHUTNI GASHNEEZ
Cilantro Chutney

Colloquially, this chutney is called *gashneetch*. It has proved very popular with all my friends. It has a sharp taste and is rich in vitamins A and C. Small amounts are served with *pakaura*, kebabs (especially *shami* kebab) and with rice dishes. It keeps fairly well in a refrigerator, although it loses some of its green color.

    8 oz fresh cilantro leaves
    ½ - 1 oz hot green chilies, seeds removed, chopped
    3 - 4 cloves garlic, peeled and chopped
    1 tbs walnuts
    1 tbs sugar
    1 cup white wine vinegar or lemon juice
    2 tsp salt
    1 tbs raisins (optional)

Grind the cilantro, green chilies, garlic and walnuts, making sure that they are mixed thoroughly. Add the sugar to the vinegar and again mix well. Add this to the cilantro mixture, with the salt and raisins if using. Mix again and put into a clean jar, screw on the lid and store in the refrigerator.

MAKES ABOUT 1 TO 2 ONE-POUND JARS

CHUTNI NAHNA
Mint Chutney

This chutney has a refreshing taste and is best made fresh when required, as it does not keep well. Serve with kebabs or rice dishes.

1 cup fresh mint leaves, washed and dried
1 - 2 cloves garlic, peeled
1 - 2 fresh green chilies, seeds removed
1 - 2 tbs yogurt
salt

Shred the mint leaves with the garlic and chilies, preferably in a food processor. Now mix in the yogurt and add salt to taste.
   Store the mint chutney covered in the refrigerator.

MAKES ONE SMALL BOWL

CHUTNI MURCH
Red Pepper Chutney

Chutni murch has a beautiful red color and has proved to be very popular with my friends. Everyone wants the recipe and here it is. It is particularly good with *qorma chalau, sambosas,* or even stirred into soups.

4 red bell peppers
1½ oz hot red chilies
1 whole head garlic
¾ cup white wine vinegar
6 tbs sugar
1 - 2 tsp salt
½ tbs *sia dona* (nigella seeds)

Wash the bell peppers, then dry them well. Seed them and chop them roughly. Seed the hot chilies and chop them roughly, taking care in handling them. Peel the cloves of garlic and roughly chop.

Place the peppers and the chilies in a blender with the garlic and blend to a thick puree. Do not blend for too long or the mixture will become too watery. Now add the vinegar, sugar and salt, adding a bit more or less of each ingredient according to taste. Last stir in the *sia dona*.

Store in clean, dry jars in a refrigerator. This chutney will keep for about a month.

MAKES ABOUT 3 ONE-POUND JARS

Fruits
and
Desserts

Desserts are considered a luxury and are usually only made for weddings, feast days, parties and other special occasions. However, this lack of "sweets" is more than made up for by the stunning variety and quality of the fruits available.

Fruit is often the only dessert and is nearly always served after the main meal of the day. In summer and autumn large bowls are filled with grapes, melons, watermelons, peaches, nectarines, pears, apples, quinces, pomegranates and plums. Melons and grapes used to be, and perhaps still are, the most abundant and there are numerous varieties of both.

Many of the grapes are made into the green and red raisins for which Afghanistan is famous (see p. 38). The green are considered to have the best flavor. Raisins, apart from being used in some Afghan dishes, are eaten alone or mixed with nuts and served with tea, especially for guests.

In winter, fruits such as oranges, bananas, lemons, tangerines and satsumas are in season. Early spring is the only time of the year when fruits are in short supply, until apricots come into season. Cucumbers are also available in late spring and, although it seemed strange to me, are often eaten as a fruit after a meal.

Mulberry and walnut trees are found mainly in northern Afghanistan. In the winter and early spring, when fruits and vegetables are scarce and expensive, a preparation of ground, dried mulberry and walnut, called *chakida*, helps supplement a somewhat deficient diet. Travelers often carry dried fruit and nut combinations tied in the end of their turban cloths. Other nuts found in Afghanistan include pistachios from the Herat region, and almonds and pine nuts. Apricot kernels are often substituted for almonds. Nuts are used in a number of Afghan dishes: in *pilaus*, desserts and pastries. Almonds coated with a sugar syrup are called *noql-e-badomi*.

MIWA NAUROZEE
New Year Fruit Compote

Miwa means fruit, and *Nauroz* the New Year. As one would expect, this compote is made for New Year celebrations. The original version was made with seven fruits, each of which had a name including the letter *seen*. So the dish may also be called *Haft* (seven) *seen* or *Haft miwa*.

The seven fruits are: *khastah,* apricot kernels; *pistah,* pistachio nuts; *kishmish surkh,* red raisins; *kishmish sabz,* green raisins; *kishmish sia* (sometimes called *monaqa),* large black raisins with seeds; *saib,* apple; and *sinjed. Sinjed* is the fruit of the *Elaeagnus* tree in the Oleaster family. It is related to the North American silverberry. It looks like a very small date, but is redder, with a large stone, a bland flavor and a mealy texture.

Tradition requires that before *Haft seen* is served, it is blessed by the reading of seven passages from the *Qo'ran,* called *Haft Salaam.* These passages are special prayers to bring health.

The ingredients now used to make *Miwa Naurozee* vary from family to family. Many use the small, sweet, dried white apricots called *shakar paura.* Almonds *(badom)* often replace apricot kernels, and walnuts *(charmaz)* are a common addition. It is fortunate that the recipe is flexible, since it can easily be made with whatever dried fruits and nuts are readily available, as in this version. I have substituted the *sinjed* with cherries.

    4 oz dried apricots
    2 oz (½ cup) light raisins
    4 oz (1 cup) red raisins
    2 oz (½ cup) walnuts
    2 oz (½ cup) pistachio nuts
    2 oz (½ cup) almonds
    2 oz (½ cup) cherries

Wash the apricots and both types of raisins and place in a bowl. Cover with cold water to 2 inches above the fruit. Cover and set aside for 2 days.

Put the walnuts, pistachios and almonds in another bowl or pan and add boiling water. Leave to soak, then peel off all the skins as they soften. This is a fiddly job, especially with the walnuts, but it is well worth the effort. Throw away the water.

After the apricots and raisins have been soaked for 2 days, combine the fruits and the juice they have been soaking in with the nuts and add the cherries. If this dish is left for a couple of days in the refrigerator the juice will become sweeter.

To serve, spoon the fruit and nuts, well mixed, and some juice into individual dishes or cups.

MAKES 6 TO 8

 **COMPOTE-E-BEHI**
Quince Compote

2 large quinces
8 oz (1 cup + 2 tbs) sugar
juice of ½ lemon
¼ tsp ground cardamom

Peel, core and cut each quince into eight pieces. Put into a pan and add water to just cover the quinces. Bring to a boil, turn down the heat and simmer until they are just soft (approximately 1 to 1½ hours). Remove the quinces with a slotted spoon from the pan and set to one side.

Now add the sugar to the pan with the water and stir to dissolve. Add the lemon juice. Bring to a boil and boil the syrup for 1 to 2 minutes. Remove from the heat, add the cardamom and return the quinces to the pan. Leave on a low heat for a little longer for the flavors to develop. The quinces should by now have become a lovely rosy pink color. Leave to cool in the syrup.

Serve with *qymaq* (p. 40) or clotted cream.

SERVES 4

FIRNI
Afghan Custard

One of the traditional sweet milky desserts, often made for special occasions, such as wedding parties and *Eid*. My family always made this dessert with cornstarch but many Afghans prefer to make it with rice flour.

6 tbs cornstarch
3½ cups milk
1¼ cups sugar
½ tsp ground green or white cardamom seeds
1 - 2 tbs finely chopped or ground pistachio
1 - 2 tbs finely chopped or ground almonds

Mix the cornstarch with a small amount of the milk to make a paste.

Heat the remaining milk in a pan and, when hot but not boiling, add the sugar. (More or less sugar may be used, according to taste). Stir well. When the milk is close to boiling, slowly add the cornstarch paste to the mixture, stirring continuously. Bring to a boil, add the cardamom, turn down the heat and simmer for about 5 minutes, stirring frequently to prevent sticking.

Pour the *firni* on to a shallow serving dish and decorate it with the pistachio and almonds and allow to cool.

Firni is always eaten cold.

SERVES 6 TO 8

 KAJKOOL-E-FUQARA
Rich Milk and Almond Dessert

The name of this rich milk and almond pudding, which is flavored with rosewater, ironically means "beggar's bowl." There are many variations of the same dessert found all over Iran and the Middle East, where it is usually known as *keshkul-e-fuqara*. The recipe below is an Afghan version.

Keshkul (*kajkool* in Dari; *kaj* means "carry" and *kool* means "shoulder") is the Persian word for an oval bowl made either of wood, metal or a coconut. These bowls were carried suspended by a chain from the shoulder by beggars or *fuqara* (*fuqara* being the plural of *faqir*).

Fuqara, who call themselves "the paupers of God," are like dervishes who devote their lives to seeking God and are not interested in ownership of property or worldly goods. They travel from house to house begging for food. Donations of food (and sometimes money, although the *faqir* cannot ask for money directly) are placed in the *keshkul/kajkool* which is eventually be filled up with different kinds of food.

A *faqir* is considered to be a holy man with special healing powers and in exchange for the food he prays for the people, often sprinkling them with rosewater from a *gul-ab-pash* which is a type of glass or metal bottle with a sprinkler. (*Gul* means "flower" in Persian, *ab* means "water" and *pash* means "sprinkle.")

The name of this rich milk dessert derives from its being sprinkled and decorated with a variety of nuts and coconut, symbolizing the *keshkul* being filled with a variety of food.

5 oz (1 cup + 2 tbs) blanched almonds
2 tbs blanched pistachio
½ fresh coconut (optional)
3 heaped tbs cornstarch
3½ cups milk
1¼ cups sugar
½ cup rosewater
½ tsp cardamom

First of all, make milk of almonds by pouring 1 cup boiling water over the cup of blanched almonds in a bowl and leave to soak for about 15 minutes. Put the almonds and their water into an electric blender and puree. Strain the almond milk through a double layer of cheesecloth or muslin into a bowl, squeezing the cloth to extract as much milk as possible. Set to one side.

Meanwhile sliver or roughly chop the remaining 2 tbs almonds and the pistachio and simmer them in a little water for a few minutes to soften. If using coconut, remove the flesh and grate. Set the almonds, pistachios and coconut to one side.

Mix the cornstarch with a little of the cold milk into a smooth paste. Bring the remaining milk to a boil with the sugar, adding the paste gradually. Stir constantly with a wooden spoon to avoid sticking. Bring to a boil, then turn down the heat and simmer gently until the mixture thickens. (It is very important not to have the heat too high and to stir constantly as this mixture easily sticks and burns. If it does stick, do not scrape the bottom of the pan as this would impart a burnt taste to the whole dish.)

Add the rosewater, milk of almonds and cardamom and simmer gently for a further 2 minutes. Leave to cool a little and then pour on to a large flat serving dish and decorate with the almonds and pistachios and coconut, if used.

SERVES 6 TO 8

MAUGHOOT
Afghan Jelly

This is made in the same way as *firni*, except that water is used instead of milk and it is flavored and colored with saffron.

6 tbs cornstarch
1¼ cups sugar
¼ tsp ground green cardamom seeds
1 tbs rosewater
¼ - ½ tsp saffron
2 tbs slivered or finely chopped pistachio
2 tbs slivered or finely chopped almonds

Mix the cornstarch with a little water to form a paste.

Heat 3½ cups water and when hot, but not boiling, add the sugar. (More or less sugar may be used, according to taste.) Stir well. When the water is close to boiling, slowly add the cornstarch paste to the liquid, stirring continuously.

Bring to a boil and add the cardamom, rosewater and saffron. Turn down the heat and boil gently for 2 to 5 minutes until the liquid becomes clear. Remove from the heat and pour onto a shallow serving dish. It should flatten out completely. Sprinkle onto it, as decoration, the pistachio and almond.

Maughoot, like *firni,* is always eaten cold.

SERVES 6 TO 8

SHEER BIRINJ
Milky Rice Pudding

Sheer birinj is, I think, similar to milky rice pudding. However, the addition of rosewater, cardamom and the nuts gives the dish a more luxurious flavor.

    4 oz (½ cup) short-grain rice
    2¼ cups milk
    ½ cup sugar
    2 tsp rosewater
    ¼ tsp ground green or white cardamom seeds
    2 tbs ground pistachio or almonds

Wash the rice and put in a pan, add 2 cups water, bring to a boil, then turn down the heat to medium and boil gently until the rice is cooked and soft and all the water has evaporated. Stir from time to time to prevent the rice from sticking.

Add the milk and bring back to a boil, then turn down the heat again and boil gently until the mixture thickens a little bit, then add the sugar. Continue to boil gently, stirring often to prevent sticking, until the sugar has dissolved and the mixture has thickened, although still runny.

Add the rosewater and ground cardamom and cook for another 1 to 2 minutes.

Serve the rice on a large flat plate, decorated with the nuts. Afghans serve this dish cold, but it can be eaten warm, if preferred.

SERVES 4 TO 6

SHOLA-E-SHIREEN
Sweet Rice with Nuts

This moist rice dish is often prepared in the lunar month of *Muharram*, for *Nauroz*, for *Eid* and for *Nazer* (see p. 10). See also *shola-e-zard* (p. 227).

    8 oz (1 cup) white short-grain rice
    ¼ cup milk
    ¾ cup sugar
    ¼ tsp saffron
    1 tbs rosewater
    ½ tsp ground green cardamom seeds
    1 - 2 tbs pistachio, skinned and chopped
    1 - 2 tbs almonds, skinned and chopped

Rinse the rice in cold water, drain it, put it into pan and add enough water to cover it by about 2 inches. Bring to a boil, cover with a lid, reduce the heat and boil gently, stirring frequently to prevent sticking, until the rice softens and the water has evaporated. This takes 20 to 30 minutes.

Add the milk, sugar and saffron. Reduce the heat to low and cover with the lid. Simmer for another 20 to 30 minutes until the rice is well cooked and soft. The rice should be moist and sticky and not too firm. Add more water if necessary to obtain the right consistency.

Add the rosewater, ground cardamom, pistachio and almond. Stir well and simmer for a few more minutes. Place on a large flat dish. Serve cold.

SERVES 4 TO 6

SHOLA-E-ZARD
Sweet Yellow Rice Pudding

Shola-e-zard is a pudding often made for *Nazer* and has particular association with the tenth day of Muharram (see p. 10) when it is traditionally served with *sharbat-e-rayhan* (basil seed shrub, see p. 278).

8 oz (1 cup) short-grain rice
1 - 1¾ cup sugar
¼ tsp saffron
1 tbs almonds, skinned and finely chopped
1 tbs pistachio, skinned and finely chopped
1 tbs rosewater
½ tsp ground green cardamom

Soak the rice in water, well covered for a couple of hours, or longer.

Boil approximately 7 cups water and add the rice. The water should come up to about 4 inches above the rice. Simmer the rice in the water slowly, stirring occasionally, until the rice dissolves and becomes like jelly. This can take 1 to 2 hours, or perhaps even longer. Add the sugar, saffron, pistachios, almonds, rosewater and ground cardamom. Turn down the heat to very low and cook for another half an hour.

Pour the warm *shola* on to a large serving dish and leave to set in a cool place for a couple of hours.

SERVES 4 TO 6

SHOLA-E-HOLBA
Sweet Rice with Fenugreek

The addition of fenugreek to flavor this rice dish is unusual. Fenu-greek is considered to be "hot" and therefore this special dessert is often prepared for people needing extra energy or nourishment, such as mothers with newborn babies.

8 oz (1 cup) short-grain rice
6 tbs butter or margarine
½ oz fenugreek
½ tsp saffron
¾ cup brown sugar

Wash the rice in cold water and drain.

Heat the butter in a pan and add the fenugreek. Stir until brown, but be careful not to burn it. Add the rice and stir well. Add enough water to cover the rice by about 2 inches, and add the saffron. Boil gently, stirring occasionally, until the rice is soft, about 30 minutes or so. You may need to add more water during the cooking, but by the end it should all have been absorbed. Add the sugar, stir again, reduce the heat, cover with a lid and simmer for half an hour. Serve either warm or cold.

SERVES 4 TO 6

DAYGCHA

Sweet, Sticky Rice Pudding

Daygcha is a thick and sticky rice dish often prepared for special ceremonies. It is cooked on the final Wednesday of the lunar month *Safar* and also for an *Eid* and birthdays. Sometimes it is served with evening tea.

8 oz (1 cup) short-grain rice
½ cup butter or margarine (preferably unsalted)
pinch of salt
2 cups milk
1 cup + 2 tbs sugar
½ tsp ground green cardamom seeds

Wash the rice. Bring 2 cups water to a boil in a pan and add the rice, the butter and salt. Boil gently, until the rice is soft. Stir occasionally during the cooking. You may have to add more water, but all the water should have been absorbed by the time the rice is cooked, about 30 to 40 minutes. Add the milk, sugar and cardamom and simmer until all the liquid evaporates and the rice is thick. Stir frequently to prevent the rice from sticking to the bottom of the pan.

Cover the pan with a cloth and then a tightly fitting lid, and leave to cook slowly over a low heat for 20 to 30 minutes. Or, better, put it in a covered casserole into a preheated oven at 300°F for the same length of time.

To serve, remove the rice to a large dish and let it cool for about 1 hour.

SERVES 6 TO 8

SHEER SEEMYAN
Vermicelli Milk Pudding

Seemyan are similar to vermicelli. A dough is made with wheat flour which is then passed through a machine which forces the dough into fine, thin strings. (*Seem* in Farsi means "silvery-white thin wire.") These are then dried and roasted in an oven.

Seemyan are usually made into puddings, which are very similar to desserts called *seviyan kheer* in India.

Seemyan can also be cooked like rice using the *sof* method and when cooked they are served sprinkled with sugar or molasses.

    3 oz vermicelli
    1 tbs ghee or vegetable oil
    2 level tbs cornstarch
    2½ cups milk
    1 cup sugar
    1 tbs rosewater
    ½ tsp ground green cardamom
    1 tbs ground pistachio (optional)

Break up the vermicelli into 2 inch lengths. Fry gently in the ghee until well coated and golden brown. Bring a pot of water to a boil and add the vermicelli. Boil gently for a couple of minutes until just soft. Drain in a colander and set to one side.

Mix the cornstarch to a paste with a little of the milk. Heat the remaining milk adding the cornstarch paste slowly and stir constantly until the milk thickens. Add the sugar, rosewater and cardamom, stir well and simmer for about 2 minutes. Now add the vermicelli to the milk, mix well and pour onto a shallow serving dish. Sprinkle with the pistachio if desired and allow to cool.

SERVES 4

SHEER YAKH
Ice Cream

Sheer yakh means "frozen milk" in Dari (the Persian dialect used in Afghanistan). Afghans have probably been making ice cream for centuries and it is possible that it was the Moghuls who took the skill of ice cream making to India. The old way of making ice cream is carried on even now in Afghanistan where refrigerators are still uncommon. Traditionally the eating and enjoyment of ice cream was a springtime treat and was made by the *sheer yakh ferosh* (ice cream seller). This man made his ice cream in a large tub-like metal cylinder which contained a smaller cylinder or bucket inside. The outer cylinder, which is stationary, is filled with salt and snow (which has been brought down in large blocks from the mountains). The inner cylinder or bucket, which has handles on top is free to rotate, is filled with milk and sugar and flavorings such as rosewater and cardamom: then it is rotated by hand by the ice cream maker. From time to time he will stop swishing the cylinder from side to side and will insert a long spoon-like pole into the gradually forming ice cream mixture and mix the ice cream from bottom to top. Then the rotating continues until the ice cream is frozen and is of a creamy texture. The ice cream is often served topped with chopped pistachios or almonds.

Sheer yakh qalebi, is another traditional ice cream which is made in cone-shaped metal molds. The same ice cream mixture is placed into these molds which have a top that is then sealed with dough before freezing.

The recipe I give below is simple and easy to make and is quite delicious. To make a richer ice cream, about ¼ cup of cream can be added and mixed in before freezing, or, you can add *sahlab* (salep, see p. 42). This does add an extra dimension to the texture of the ice cream—it gives it a more elastic and smooth texture. Sprinkle one level teaspoon on the milk and sugar mixture before freezing and beat in until dissolved.

Flavorings can be varied, as can toppings, such as *qymaq*.

¾ cup sugar
2¼ cups whole milk
2 - 3 tbs ground pistachio or almonds
1 -2 tbs rosewater or orange flower water
¼ tsp ground cardamom

Chill the ice cream maker according to the manufacturer's instructions.

Add the sugar to the milk and stir well until completely dissolved. Add 2 tbs of the ground pistachio and 1 tablespoon of the rosewater. Mix well, then pour into the ice cream maker and freeze, again according to the manufacturer's instructions.

To serve, sprinkle with the remaining flavorings and chopped nuts, and perhaps some *qymaq*.

SERVES ABOUT 4

 **FALUDA**

Faluda is a type of sweet noodle dessert or drink which dates back to ancient times and variations occur in Iran, India and indeed, all over the Near and Middle East. In Iran it is called *paloodeh* and in India *falooda*. A relative of this dish called *balooza* is prepared in other parts of the Middle East.

Cornstarch or wheatstarch and water are blended together and then cooked over heat until the mixture becomes a translucent paste. In Afghanistan this starch is made by soaking whole wheat grains which are then ground with water yielding a milky liquid called *nishaste*. This is then cooked and the warm paste is forced through a type of colander or pasta machine (in India this is called a *seviyan* machine), into iced water. The result is that tiny rice-like grains or small vermicelli are formed in the ice. In Afghanistan these rice-like grains are called *jhala*, which means hail stones, because of their resemblance to hail. The *jhala* are served with a fruit drink or syrup, or as a topping for ice cream, *qymaq, firni* or a milk pudding flavored and thickened with *salep*, all with a final sprinking of rosewater.

Mounstuart Elphinstone in his book *An Account of the Kingdom of Caubul*, wrote in the early nineteenth century of *faluda*:

> Ice, or rather snow, is to be had in Caubul, during the summer, for a mere trifle . . . A favourite food at that season is fulodeh, a jelly strained from boiled wheat, and eaten with the expressed juice of fruits and ice, to which cream also is sometimes added.

Here is a recipe for you to try.

6 tbs cornstarch or wheatstarch
iced water
ice cream
qymaq or clotted cream (p. 40)
rosewater

Blend together the cornstarch with ¼ cup water to make a smooth paste. Then slowly add 1 cup of water. Heat this in a pan very gently, stirring continuously until a smooth thick paste is formed. When the mixture becomes translucent remove from the heat and when the paste is cool enough to handle, place a colander over a bowl of ice-cold water and press the paste through the colander. The paste will form into opaque and firm vermicelli-like strings (*jhala*). Alternatively, place the paste in an icing bag and force the paste through the nozzle into the iced water to form vermicelli-like *jhala*.

Strain the *jhala* and serve on top of ice cream, with perhaps some *qymaq* and a sprinkling of rosewater.

SERVES ABOUT 4

🐘 HALWA-E-AURDI
Wheat Halva

Of the many forms which *halwa* takes, the most traditional ones in Afghanistan are made with cereals, such as wheat, semolina and rice flour. However, other kinds are made, for example those based on vegetables such as carrot and beet.

Generally, the *halwa* prepared in Afghanistan are closely related to the other *halva* desserts, which are popular throughout the Near East, Central Asia and India.

Halwa, especially the cereal version, is served at many festive celebrations, but it is also served at funerals and is made for *Nazer* (p. 10). It is mildly sweet and delicately flavored. Nuts are added to the finest *halwa,* as in this recipe, but it is often made without them.

> ¾ cup sugar
> 6 oz (12 tbs) margarine or vegetable fat
> 8 oz (1¾ cup) *chapati* or wheat-meal flour
> 1 tbs pistachio, slivered
> 1 tbs almonds, slivered
> ½ tsp ground green cardamom seeds
> 1 tsp rosewater (optional)

Mix the sugar with 1 cup water.

Melt the margarine over a medium to high heat, add the flour slowly, and stir and fry, stirring continuously, until it turns a golden brown color. Next, add the sugar mixture to the flour mixture, again stirring continuously; then add another 1 cup water and mix gently with a spoon. The fat will separate out. Continue cooking until the water has evaporated, at which point the pistachio, almonds, cardamom, and rosewater (if used) are put in. Cover with a lid and put into a preheated oven at 300°F for half an hour.

Serve *halwa* slightly warm, or cold, in a large dish or bowl, or in individual dessert dishes.

SERVES 6 TO 8

VARIATION:
HALWA-E-AURD-E-BIRINJI
Ground Rice Halva

This *halwa* is made in exactly the same way as *halwa-e-aurdi,* except that ground rice replaces the flour and the finished dish is white, rather than brown. Also, rosewater is more commonly used in flavoring; and the amount should be increased to 2 teaspoons. *Halwa-e-aurd-e-birinji* has a finer and more delicate flavor and texture than ordinary *halwa-e-aurdi.*

VARIATION:
HALWA-E-AURD-E-SUJEE
Semolina Halva

This is the same as *halwa-e-aurdi* except that it is made with semolina, not flour.

HALWA-E-ZARDAK
Carrot Halva

1 lb carrots
6 tbs vegetable oil
1½ cups milk
½ cup sugar
1 tbs pistachio, chopped into quarters
1 tbs almonds, chopped into quarters
1 - 2 tbs raisins (or sultanas)
½ tsp ground green cardamom seeds

Shred or grate the carrots and drain off any liquid. Heat 5 tablespoons of the oil, and stir in the shredded carrots until they begin to brown and any water has evaporated. Add the milk and sugar, stir well, then reduce the heat and simmer for about an hour, stirring occasionally. All the liquid should have evaporated and the oil will have separated out.

Fry the nuts and raisins in the remaining 1 tablespoon of oil until they are lightly browned and the raisins have swollen up. Add to the cooked carrot. Add the ground cardamom. Mix well and leave for a further 2 minutes or so on a low heat.

Serve warm or cold.

SERVES 4

 **LEETEE**

My husband's aunty, Gul Jan Kabiri, gave me this recipe. *Leetee* is a special dish prepared for mothers who have just given birth. It is considered to be a "hot" food and therefore nourishing and strengthening. For people with a sweet tooth a little more sugar can be added.

4 oz (½ cup) butter, ghee or oil
8 oz (1¾ cups) all-purpose flour or white chapati flour
6 tbs sugar
¼ tsp saffron threads soaked in a little warm water
1 tsp ground cardamom
1 tsp cinnamon
4 tbs chopped raisins, almonds, walnuts and pistachios

Heat the butter in a pan. Slowly sift in the flour, stirring constantly. Continue stirring and fry until the flour becomes golden in color, taking care not to burn it. Remove from the heat and slowly add about 2¼ cups cold water, stirring all the time until the mixture is the consistency of a thick custard. Stir in the sugar (more or less, according to taste), and add the liquid saffron, cardamom and cinnamon. Heat again and cook gently for 2 to 3 minutes.

Serve warm or hot in small soup bowls and sprinkle generously with the chopped raisins and nuts.

SERVES 6 TO 8

KACHEE
Halva Cream

Another ancient recipe, similar to *leetee* (see p. 236), prepared for mothers who have just given birth to strengthen and nourish them. It is a popular warming winter dish.

8 oz (1 cup) butter or ghee
8 oz (1¾ cups) all-purpose white flour
pinch of salt
2 tbs rosewater (optional)
½ cup sugar, preferably brown, or molasses

Melt 12 tablespoons of the butter in a pan and gradually stir in the flour, mixing to a smooth paste. Now add about 4 cups water, little by little, stirring continuously until a consistency like thick custard is formed. Add a pinch of salt, and the rosewater if used. Cook for a couple more minutes, still stirring continuously.

Finally, pour the *kachee* on to a serving dish and make a well in the center. Melt the remaining 4 tablespoons butter and pour into the well. Sprinkle the whole liberally with the brown sugar.

Serve hot.

SERVES 4

MOLIDA
Wedding Sweetmeat

This is perhaps the most traditional food served at weddings. The *molida*, or *changali*, as it is sometimes called, is tasted by the bride and groom as they sit on their wedding throne. The groom first feeds his bride a teaspoonful of *molida*, then she in turn feeds him with a teaspoonful. The *molida* is then served to the wedding guests.

    1½ lbs (5¼ cups) brown *chapati* flour
    5 tbs vegetable oil
    1 pkt quick rise yeast
    a good pinch of salt
    1¼ cups warm water
    3 level tbs ground cardamom
    1¼ cup superfine sugar
    1 tbs rosewater
    3½ oz (7 tbs) melted butter or ghee

Make a dough with the flour, oil, yeast and salt in the same way as for making *nan* (see p. 47), cover with a damp cloth and leave to rise in a warm place for about half an hour. Preheat the oven to 450°F.

Form the dough into four rounds of about 1 inch thick. Brush a baking tray with a little oil and place the four rounds of dough on it. Then bake in the preheated oven for about 20 minutes or until well risen and golden brown.

Allow the bread to cool, then make into fine breadcrumbs, either by crumbling in your hands or in a food processor. Now add the ground cardamom and the sugar. Sprinkle with the rosewater and mix well. Next slowly drizzle the melted butter over the mixture and mix in well making sure to keep the crumbs fine and not sticking together.

Pile the *molida* on a large plate, each guest helping themselves onto smaller plates.

SERVES 6 TO 8

Pastries, Sweets and Biscuits

Rich pastries, cakes, biscuits and sweets are, on the whole, considered a luxury and only usually served for special occasions or for guests. They are rarely made in the home as few families have facilities for baking and some of them require expertise. They are, therefore, often bought from local bakeries called *kulcha feroshee*.

Many of the pastries are similar to those found in other countries of the Middle East, Central Asia and India.

NAN-E-PARATA
Sweet Fried Bread

1¼ lbs (4⅓ cups) all-purpose flour, sifted
1½ tsp salt
1 pkt quick rise yeast
10 oz (1¼ cups) lukewarm water
12 tbs oil, plus more for deep-frying
½ cup confectioners' sugar

Sift the flour with the salt and mix in the yeast. Add the water a little at a time and mix to form a firm dough. Knead the dough until it is smooth and elastic, shape it into a ball and leave it, covered, in a bowl for about half an hour.

Divide the dough into 4 balls, and again divide each of these into 4, making 16 altogether.

On a lightly floured board roll each ball in turn into a disc no thicker than ¹⁄₁₆ inch. Then, using a pastry brush, brush 1 tablespoon of oil over 3 discs and stack them on top of each other topping with a fourth. Press down lightly with a rolling pin. Each stack should not be more than ¼ inch thick. Repeat, making four breads in all.

Heat enough vegetable oil in a large frying pan to deep-fry and fry the breads over a medium to high heat, one at a time, until light brown. They should not be too crisp. Remove and drain. Sift the sugar over the hot breads, on both sides.

Smaller breads can be made, but this size is traditional.

MAKES 4

GOASH-E-FEEL
"Elephant's Ear" Pastry

"Elephant's ear" is the literal meaning of *goash-e-feel*, a name given because of the shape and size of these crisp, bubbly, sweet pastries. Street vendors often sell them on New Year's Day (*Nauroz*) or festivals. Traditionally they are also made on the day after a wedding when the bride's family sends them to the bride and groom.

For the best results, the pastry must be rolled out paper thin, and the oil for frying must be hot.

```
1 egg
1 tbs oil or melted butter
milk
8 oz (1¾ cup) flour
salt
¼ - ½ cup confectioners' sugar vegetable oil for frying
1 - 2 tbs ground pistachio
```

Break the egg into a bowl, beat it, and add the melted butter. Now add enough milk to make the liquid measure ½ cup. Sift the flour with a pinch of salt and 1 tsp of confectioners' sugar. Add to the egg and milk mixture and mix well to form a firm dough. Knead on a lightly floured surface or board for about 10 minutes until smooth and elastic. Divide the dough into 8 equal balls, cover with a moistened cloth and set to one side in a cool place for about half an hour.

On a lightly floured board, roll out each of the 8 balls until paper thin; they should be approximately 7 inches in diameter. Shape the "ears" by pleating one side of each piece of dough. Nip together with wet fingers, to prevent the pleats from opening during frying.

In a frying pan of similar diameter, heat enough oil to shallow-fry the pastries. When the oil is hot, put in the "ears" one at a time and fry on both sides until golden brown. As you remove the pastries from the pan, shake off the excess oil gently or place on paper towels. Now sprinkle the pastries on both sides with a mixture of sifted confectioners' sugar and ground pistachio.

There are many variations of *goash-e-feel*, so do not feel limited as to the size and shapes you can make. Some Afghans make what is called *goash-e-asp* ("horse's ear") or bow knots.

MAKES 8

 KULCHA-E-PANJEREI
"Window" Biscuits

I first remember eating these delicate and light biscuits in Kunduz, northern Afghanistan when my husband's cousin, Mahgul Hachimzada, showed me how to make them. You will need a fritter iron. They come in various shapes. I have one in the shape of a butterfly and one in the shape of a flower.

    2 medium eggs
    1 tsp sugar
    ¼ tsp salt
    4 oz (¾ cup + 2 tbs) all-purpose flour
    8 oz (1 cup) milk
    2 tsp butter, melted
    oil for frying
    confectioners' sugar for dusting

Beat the eggs in a bowl until well blended. Add and mix in well the sugar and salt then gradually stir in the flour alternately with the milk and the melted butter. Beat well.

Heat about 4 inches oil in a deep pan or fryer to 400°F. Immerse the fritter iron in the hot oil to season. Then dip it in the batter, making sure the batter does not cover the top of the iron. Immerse quickly in the hot oil for 20 to 30 seconds, until the bubbles disappear and the biscuit is golden brown. Remove the fritter carefully from the iron, if necessary with a fork, and drain. Repeat until all the batter is used up. When cool, dust with confectioners' sugar. These are best served immediately and do not store well.

MAKES 40 TO 50

🌀 QATLAMA

A sweet fried pastry, more common in northern Afghanistan, which can be a bit fiddly to make. This recipe gives the traditional way of making *qatlama*. However, smaller shapes—triangular, square or diamond—can be made and five or six layers of pastry instead of seven can be used.

2 eggs
1 lb (3½ cups) all-purpose flour
pinch of salt
½ tsp baking powder
2 tbs margarine, melted or vegetable oil
½ cup milk or water
4 tbs vegetable oil, and more for deep-frying
½ cup confectioners' sugar
2 - 3 tbs ground pistachio

Beat the eggs in a mixing bowl until they foam.

Sift the flour, salt and baking powder together into a large mixing bowl. Make a well and add the eggs and the margarine. Gradually add the milk (more or less, as needed) and mix to form a stiff dough. Knead for about 5 to 10 minutes until the dough is firm and elastic. Shape the dough into a ball, cover the bowl with a cloth and leave to stand for about half an hour.

Divide the dough into 4 balls, then roll each out, on a lightly floured board, as thinly as possible: aim for a diameter of about 12 to 14 inches. Cut each into 4-inch squares. With the 4 tablespoons of melted margarine brush each square with a pastry brush and put the squares one on top of the other in piles of seven. Fold each seven-layered pile into a triangle, and press down gently with a rolling pin.

In a deep pan, heat enough oil for deep-frying and fry the pastries until golden brown. Remove from the oil, shaking off excess oil and while still hot sprinkle with a mixture of sifted confectioners' sugar and ground pistachio.

Serve warm or cold.

MAKES ABOUT 5

🌸 SAMBOSA SHIREEN
Sweet Stuffed Pastries

Afghans like to make a sweet variation of *sambosa*. This is the same recipe as for *sambosa goshti*, except that the pastry squares are filled with *halwa-e-aurd-e-sujee* or *halwa-e-aurd-e-birinji*. Filo pastry can be substituted.

> *halwa* made with 8 oz semolina or rice flour (p. 235)
> 1 lb (450 g) *sambosa* dough made with 1 lb flour (p. 72)
> confectioners' sugar, sifted
> 1 tbs ground pistachio (optional)
> vegetable oil for deep-frying

Prepare the *halwa*.

Prepare the pastry as for *sambosa goshti*. Roll out the pastry as thinly as possible and cut into 4-inch squares.

Place 1 tablespoon of the *halwa* on each square. Fold the squares to make triangles and seal the edges tightly.

(If using ready-made filo pastry, cut into strips of 4 inches by about 6 inches, brush 6 layers with oil and place on top of each other. Place the filling of your choice and then fold up into a triangle shape.)

Heat vegetable oil in a frying pan, deep-fry the *sambosa* until golden brown on both sides. Remove from the oil and drain.

Alternatively brush generously with oil and bake in a preheated oven at 325°F for 20 to 30 minutes until golden brown.

Dust the warm pastries with a little confectioners' sugar and ground pistachio if used.

Sambosa shireen are usually served with tea, either hot or cold.

MAKES ABOUT 24

VARIATION:
Fill the pastry squares with a filling of fruit and nuts as follows:

> 4 oz (¾ cup) raisins, very finely chopped or ground
> 4 oz (¾ cup) walnuts or almonds, finely chopped or ground
> 1 tsp sugar
> 1 tsp cinnamon
> 1 tbs hot water

Combine the fruit and nuts, add the sugar and cinnamon and mix in a little hot water. Mix well, then proceed as for the main recipe above adding about 1 to 2 tsp of the filling on each square.

BAQLAWA
Sweet Pastry with Nuts

This sweet pastry is similar to the *baqlava* of other countries of the Middle East and Central Asia. If you make your own filo pastry it can require a fair amount of preparation time. I find it much easier to buy ready-made filo pastry, which is now readily available either frozen or fresh, from many supermarkets or delicatessens.

　1 lb filo pastry
　vegetable oil
　2 cups ground walnuts or almonds
　1 cup ground pistachio

　FOR THE SYRUP:
　2¼ cups sugar
　2 tbs lemon juice
　¼ tsp saffron
　2 tbs rosewater
　½ tsp ground green cardamom seeds

Prepare a baking tray approximately 14 × 8 × 2 inches by oiling generously.

　Brush each of 6 sheets of filo pastry with oil and lay them on top of each other in the baking tray, then sprinkle the top layer with about a third of the ground walnuts and a quarter of the ground pistachio. Repeat this whole process twice, so that you have an 18-layer pile and a quarter of the pistachio nuts remain for sprinkling over the cooked pastry. Oil the last sheets of pastry and place on top of the pile, brushing the top generously with any remaining oil.

Using a sharp knife cut carefully through all the layers length-wise to form strips of about 1½ inches wide; then cut diagonally across these to form diamond-shaped pieces. Put these in a pre-heated oven at 325°F for 35 to 45 minutes until golden brown on top.

Just before the pastry is ready to come out of the oven make the syrup. Put the sugar, 1 cup water, lemon juice and saffron in a pan and bring to a boil slowly to dissolve the sugar. Boil gently for a few minutes until it becomes syrupy and will coat the back of a spoon. Add the rosewater and cardamom and simmer for another couple of minutes. Keep warm.

Remove the pastry from the oven and spoon the warm syrup over until all of it is used and the pastry is well covered. Sprinkle the reserved ground pistachio on top and then leave to cool before serving.

MAKES ABOUT 30

 JELABI

Jelabi are usually eaten as a sweet in winter after eating fish. It was a common sight in winter for us to see the fish in the bazaars displayed alongside mountains of *jelabi*. They are also prepared for engaged couples and by tradition the groom's family send them with fish to the bride's family on New Year's Day.

I have found *jelabi* difficult to make and I have to confess that I have not been successful in making them in perfect shapes. The recipe has been given to me by my sister-in-law, who makes them without any problem. She tells me that the secret lies in the oil being the right temperature and a steady, firm and confident hand in squeezing out the batter into the oil.

1 level tbs baking powder
1¼ cups warm water
1 tbs yogurt
8 oz (1¾ cups) all-purpose flour
oil for deep-frying

FOR THE SYRUP:
8 oz (1 cup + 2 tbs) sugar
pinch of saffron
few drops of rosewater

Add the baking powder to ¼ cup of the warm water and mix. Add the yogurt and then leave in the oven, preheated to its lowest setting, for about 15 minutes.

Make a thick batter by beating the flour and the remaining 1 cup of warm water. Add the yogurt mixture. Cover with a thick, clean cloth and leave the batter to rise in a warm place for about 1 to 2 hours.

Now make the syrup. Dissolve the sugar in the 1 cup water, add the saffron and rosewater. Boil over a high heat until the syrup thickens, 5 to 6 minutes. Remove from the heat but keep warm in a bowl over a pan of hot water.

In a deep pan, heat the oil to a temperature of 350°F for deep-frying. Pour the batter into a piping bag fitted with a fine nozzle and pipe straight onto the hot oil a spiral of three circles and then form two straight lines across. This has to be done quickly and may need practice. Fry until golden brown, then remove from the oil carefully with tongs or a perforated spoon and dip into the warm syrup, coating both sides. Leave to cool on a separate tray dish. Repeat until all the batter is used up.

Making jelabi.

KHAJOOR or BOSRAUQ
Fried Cakes

The shape of these small fried cakes varies from family to family. When made in the traditional way, *khajoor* are pressed over a wire strainer or sieve which gives a mesh-like imprint. Many people do not caramelize the sugar, as in this recipe, but add it directly to the mixture of flour and salt.

½ tbs dried yeast
½ cup warm water
4¼ cups all-purpose flour
½ tsp salt
½ cup vegetable oil or margarine
1 cup + 2 tbs sugar
vegetable oil for frying

Combine the yeast with the warm water and set aside to soften.
    Sift the flour and salt together in a large mixing bowl.
    In a pan, melt the oil and sugar together. Pour quickly into the flour and stir rapidly to prevent the formation of large sugar crystals as the caramelized sugar cools. Then add the yeast mixture and the ½ cup cold water and mix to make a firm dough. Do not allow it to stand, but at once take a little of the mixture and form it into a ball about the size of an egg. Flatten this against the convex surface of a sieve to a thickness of about ⅛ inch and a diameter of about 2 inches, then roll it up loosely and seal (see the drawing on opposite page).
    Fry the cakes in deep oil until golden brown, remove, drain well and cool.

MAKES ABOUT 50

KULCHA-E-NAUROZEE or KULCHA-E-BIRINJI
Ground Rice Biscuits

These biscuits are often called *kulcha Naurozee* because they are specially made for the New Year celebrations, but they are also sometimes made for other festive occasions.

8 oz (1 cup) margarine or vegetable oil
2 cups confectioners' sugar
1 egg white
8 oz ground rice
3½ cups all-purpose flour
1 tsp baking powder
1 - 2 tsp ground pistachio

If using margarine, melt over a low heat and allow to cool.

Mix the sugar, margarine and egg white. Sift together the rice, flour and baking powder, and gradually add to the sugar and margarine mixture, stirring well all the time. Then gently knead until the mixture forms a stiff, smooth dough.

Take a piece of nonstick parchment paper about 6 by 6 inches and gently roll out on it a piece of dough the size of an egg into a 6-inch round. Score the biscuit with a fork, forming parallel lines down the biscuit.

Repeat until all the dough has been used up.

Place the biscuits on the parchment papers on baking trays and bake in a preheated oven at 300°F for 45 minutes. The biscuits should not brown. About 10 minutes before the end of baking time, sprinkle the biscuits lightly with ground pistachio.

Remove from the oven, allow to cool.

Serve the biscuits on the parchment paper.

MAKES ABOUT 12

AB-E-DANDON
"Melt-in-the-Mouth" Biscuits

These were my favorite biscuits in Afghanistan. They are light and crumbly. They are made all year-round but are especially popular for New Year (*Nauroz*) on 21 March. Aziza Ashraf has kindly given me this recipe. They are not too difficult to make, the only snag being that Aziza recommends that for best results the dough should be kneaded for about an hour! Some Afghans call them *khetaye*.

    3 cups all-purpose flour
    1 cup confectioners' sugar
    1½ tsp baking powder
    ½ tsp ground cardamom
    1¼ cups vegetable oil
    1 tbs rosewater
    1 - 2 tsp ground pistachio

Preheat the oven to 400°F.

Sift the flour, sugar, baking power and the cardamom together in a bowl. Warm the oil in a pan and then slowly mix into the flour mixture. Add the rosewater. Work and knead thoroughly for at least half an hour. Cover and leave to rest for about half an hour.

Form the dough into round balls about the size of a large walnut. Make an indent in the center with your thumb.

Place the biscuits onto a greased baking sheet and cook in the oven for 10 to 12 minutes. Do not let the biscuits brown—they should remain pale and the top should crack and be crumbly.

Remove from the oven, sprinkle with the ground pistachio nut and allow to cool. These biscuits keep well in an airtight tin or container.

MAKES 12 TO 14

KULCHA-E-NAMAKI
Savory Biscuits

1 lb (3½ cups) all-purpose or *chapati* flour
1 tsp baking powder
1 tsp salt
8 oz (1 cup) margarine
½ cup milk
egg yolk for glazing
sia dona (nigella seeds), sesame seeds and aniseed for
    sprinkling

Sift the flour, baking powder and salt into a bowl and then rub in the margarine until the mixture resembles bread crumbs. Add the milk gradually and mix gently to form a dough. Leave to stand for half an hour.

Form a piece of the dough into a size and shape slightly larger than a Ping Pong ball. Roll out on a lightly floured board to a thickness of ⅛ inch. Repeat with all the dough. (Alternatively, the dough can be rolled out and the biscuits cut out with a pastry cutter.) Prick the biscuits all over with a fork, then brush with beaten egg yolk. Sprinkle with the seeds.

Bake the biscuits on a greased baking tray(s) in an oven preheated to 400°F until golden brown for 15 to 20 minutes.

These biscuits are often eaten at tea time, along with sweet ones.

MAKES ABOUT **15**

SHEER PAYRA
Milk and Sugar Sweet

This rich sweet is served with tea on special occasions such as the birth of a baby. It is important not to boil the syrup for too long as the sweet will become rock hard. Variations can be made: for example instead of walnuts you can use almonds or pistachios. A little saffron added will color the sweets golden yellow.

2¼ cups sugar
8 oz (1 cup) dry powdered milk
1 tsp rosewater
2 tbs walnuts, finely chopped
½ tsp ground white or green cardamom seeds
1 tbs ground or finely chopped pistachio

Grease or oil a baking tin or dish which is approximately 8 × 8 inches and 1½ inches deep.

Mix the sugar with 10 tablespoons water in a pan, stir over a high heat until dissolved, then boil for 1 to 2 minutes until syrupy (the "smooth" stage, when a little of the syrup placed on a cold saucer will not run but becomes white and congealed). When this stage is reached, quickly remove from the heat and add the powdered milk, slowly and mixing well. The mixture will thicken. Stir in the rosewater, walnuts and ground cardamom.

Put the mixture immediately into the prepared tin or dish. Sprinkle with pistachio and leave to cool and set slightly for a minute or so, then before completely set cut the mixture into diamond or square shapes of about 1½ × 1½ inches with a greased, sharp knife. Leave for 2 hours in a cool place or refrigerator.

MAKES ABOUT 25

ABRAYSHUM KEBAB
Silk Kebab

An ancient dish, which is usually only made for festive occasions such as weddings. It is really a sort of sweet omelette, but cooked in an extraordinary way so that, as the name implies, the finished products seem to be made of silken threads in a kebab-like shape. The word *abrayshum* means "silk" and comes from the Persian verb *reshidan*, "to spin."

Preparation is fairly difficult and varies from family to family. I have used the method my sister-in-law taught me. She also suggests serving this sweet with ice cream. It is an ideal partnership. The crisp, sweet kebabs marry well with the creamy smooth texture of the ice cream. The number of kebabs made will depend on the size of your frying pan.

One other thing I should mention, apart from the difficulty of making this kebab, is that as you string the egg vigorously over the frying pan, egg can go everywhere and it is a bit messy.

1 cup sugar
½ tbs lemon juice
½ tsp ground cardamom seeds
pinch of saffron
½ tbs rosewater (optional)
5 eggs
vegetable oil for frying
1 - 2 tbs ground pistachio

Add the sugar to 1 cup water in a pan with the lemon juice and bring to a boil, stirring gently until the sugar has dissolved. Boil vigorously for 5 to 10 minutes until you have a syrup of a consistency which will coat the back of a metal spoon. Next add the ground cardamom, saffron, and rosewater. Boil a minute or two more. Set to one side.

Whisk the eggs in a bowl until smooth but not frothy.

Heat the oil until hot in a frying pan about 1 inch deep. Then reduce the heat slightly to medium/high. The temperature of the oil is important and this may take a little while to get just right.

The oil should be hot enough to just set and cook through the egg. (If the temperature is too high, the eggs will cook too quickly and go brown. If not hot enough the eggs will not cook through and you may get egg blobs rather than "silken" threads!)

The next procedure may need a little practice and may at first not work perfectly, but persevere.

With fingers widespread dip them into the egg mixture and then rapidly string the egg across the hot oil making threads of silk. Try to make the threads as fine as possible. Repeat the process but change direction to form a crisscross of egg threads. Continue three or four times until the surface of the oil is covered with a mesh or web of "silk" fabric. This should be done as quickly as possible as the egg cooks and becomes a golden color fairly quickly.

A new tip given to me by Fatima Gailani for making this kebab is to use a metal or plastic pan scrubber instead of fingers! This helps the eggs threads to be made more finely and evenly and I have found that it is an easier and quicker method.

Now take a skewer and loosen the "threads" around the edge of the pan. Then take the skewer and, starting at the edge of the pan nearest to you, skewer through the threads. Hold the other skewer on top and by turning the skewers around each other, roll up the threads to form a roll about 1 inch in diameter. Holding the kebab carefully on the skewers, drain off excess oil and carefully remove it onto a dish.

Repeat this process until all the egg mixture has been used up.

Over each kebab now spoon about 2 to 3 tablespoons of the prepared syrup and sprinkle generously with ground pistachio and more cardamom, if wished.

While the kebab is still warm it can be cut up into 2 or 3 portions.

MAKES ABOUT 9 TO 12

NOQL-E-BADOMI
Sugared Almonds

These sweets are traditionally served on festive occasions such as engagements or weddings. They are, however, often served with tea, especially for guests. They are not easy to make, and Afghans usually buy them from the bazaar to save themselves the trouble.

It is very important to prepare the syrup correctly and, when coating the almonds, to shake the pan vigorously. If the syrup is boiled for too long, the almonds will stick together; if not boiled for long enough, it will not become white. The coating will not be smooth, as with commercial sugared almonds, but uneven and bubbly.

Noql can also be made with roasted chickpeas (*noql-e-nakhodi*) or apricot or peach kernels (*noql-e-khastahi*).

1 lb almonds
2¼ cups sugar
½ - 1 tsp ground white or green cardamom seeds

First of all roast the almonds in a preheated oven at 300°F for about 5 minutes or so until golden.

While the almonds are roasting, warm 1 cup water in a pan. Add the sugar and cardamom to the warm water, dissolve the sugar over a medium to high heat, then boil for a couple of minutes until syrupy (the "smooth" stage, when a little of the syrup, put on a cold saucer, does not run but becomes white and congealed). At this point, reduce the heat. Meanwhile put half of the almonds in a large pan. Taking one spoonful of the syrup at a time, pour it over the almonds and shake the pan vigorously in order to coat the almonds completely. (If two people do this together it is easier: one to pour, one to shake.) Continue until all the almonds in the pan are covered and white, then repeat with the remaining almonds.

LADOO
Chickpea Sweetmeat

My husband remembers these sweets being sold by street vendors in Afghanistan. They are also a common sweet in India and it was in Jack Santa Maria's book, *Indian Sweet Cookery* where I found several recipes. I have adapted one of them to re-create the *ladoo* my husband remembers.

4 tbs ghee or butter
8 oz (1¾ cups) chickpea (besan) flour
6 cardamoms, skinned and crushed
1 cup + 2 tbs brown sugar
2 tbs ground or finely chopped pistachio nuts
milk, if necessary

Heat and melt the ghee, then gradually add the flour. Fry until golden. Remove from the heat and add the cardamom, sugar and nuts. Mix well, allow to cool and form into balls, the size of a small egg or a walnut, with the help of a little extra ghee or butter on the hands. If the mixture is too crumbly a little milk can be added to the mixture to help with the binding.

SERVES 4 TO 6

HALWA-E-SWANAK
Nut Brittle

A kind of hard toffee, usually made for special occasions such as an *Eid*. Afghans usually make quite large *halwa-e swanak* but any size can be made. This recipe, given to me by my sister-in-law, is for small ones, which are easier to prepare.

¼ cup granulated sugar
2 tbs vegetable oil
1 heaped tbs all-purpose flour
1 - 2 tbs walnuts or pistachio, ground or finely chopped

Put the sugar in a pan over a medium to high heat. Stir vigorously until it melts and turns golden brown, and a froth appears on top of it. Then carefully add the oil, stirring vigorously as you do so. Turn down the heat to low and add the flour, a little at a time, stirring quickly all the time. Add the chopped nuts. Continue stirring for 1 minute. Then, using a warmed tablespoon, remove a spoonful of the mixture. If it is still too hot to handle, wait a minute or so until it has cooled down a bit, then form it into a round ball. Work quickly as, if the mixture cools down too much, it will be difficult to mold. Flatten the ball and roll out into a round shape to a thickness of about ⅛ inch. Repeat until all the mixture has been used up. Leave to cool.

MAKES 5 TO 6

KHASTA-E-SHIREEN
Caramelized Nuts

Khasta means "nut" or "kernel" and *shireen* means "sweet." The large round plates of caramelized almond or apricot kernels are a common sight in the bazaars and are a special treat, especially for children, at festival times such as *Nauroz* (New Year) and *Eid*. Large chunks are broken off and munched on.

    8 oz almonds
    oil
    1 cup + 2 tbs granulated sugar

Roast the almonds on a baking try in a preheated oven at 300°F, for 5 minutes or so until golden brown.

Remove from the oven. Brush a nonstick baking tray (a round tray if you have one, about 10 inches in diameter) with a little oil. Spread the almonds in one layer over it.

Place the sugar in a pan and stir constantly over a very low heat until the sugar has melted and becomes light brown caramel color. While still hot pour it carefully over the nuts so that when it cools they will stick together as the caramel hardens.

Another method is to add the nuts to the caramelized sugar, stir until all are well coated and then spread out quickly over an oiled baking tray as flatly as possible.

SERVES 4

Jams
and
Conserves

Jams and conserves called *muraba* in Afghanistan are more like compotes or fruits in syrup than the thick set jams of the West. Although they can be eaten like jam on bread they are more often enjoyed as a dessert, spooned over yogurt or ice cream, or stirred into rice pudding (rather like I remember from my own childhood).

Muraba are made with a variety of fruits and vegetables, ranging from the well known ones in the West such as oranges, apples and cherries to the not so well known, quince, carrot, ginger and pumpkin. Every housewife guarded her own secret recipes, proudly serving her very own special or unusual jam to her guests.

 **MURABA-E-BEHI**
Quince Jam

This recipe comes from my husband's grandmother who was renowned for her culinary skills. He remembers her making this jam when he was a little boy.

   2 large quinces
   2 oranges
   4½ cups sugar
   1 tbs lemon juice
   1 tsp cardamom
   1 tbs rosewater

Peel and core the quinces and cut into thin slices or small cubes. Peel the oranges with a potato peeler, leaving behind the pith and cut the peel into julienne strips.

Place the quinces and the orange peel in a pan with 3¾ cups water. Bring to a boil, then reduce the heat and boil gently until the quinces are soft, about 40 to 45 minutes. Now add the sugar and increase the heat until all the sugar has dissolved. Add the lemon juice and cardamom and boil gently until the mixture has thickened and is syrupy. The quinces will have turned a lovely rosy pink/red color. Add the rosewater and leave to cool before placing in bottles or jars.

MAKES ABOUT 2 TO 3 ONE-POUND JARS

VARIATION:
Omit the orange peel and instead, just before placing the lids on the jars, place a walnut half on top of the jam.

MURABA-E-ZARDAK
Carrot Jam

The green pistachios and white almonds in this jam contrast beautifully with the rich velvety orange of the carrots and look like sparkling jewels. It also tastes good, especially when served with yogurt as a dessert, and it is delicious on bread.

1 lb carrots
2¾ cups sugar
½ cup slivered almonds
½ cup slivered pistachios
5 tbs lemon juice
2 tsp ground cardamom
2 tbs rosewater

Scrape, wash and shred or grate the carrots.
Add the sugar to 1¼ cups water in a pan and bring to a boil, stir to dissolve the sugar. Now add the carrots, almonds, pistachios, lemon juice, cardamom and rosewater and bring back to a boil. Boil vigorously for about 15 minutes until the mixture is syrupy.
Cool a little before placing in clean, dry warm jars. Allow to cool completely before sealing with a lid. Store in a cool place.

MAKES ABOUT 2 ONE-POUND JARS

MURABA-E-SAIB
Apple Jam

Afghans usually enjoy eating this jam, which is actually more like a compote, as a dessert with yogurt. Royal Gala apples are good for this recipe. The apple should not become mushy but remain in firm slices. It does not really matter if the syrup does not set like jam and, whether or not you use cardamom or rosewater, this dessert is quite delicious.

> 5 - 10 cardamom pods, or 1 tbs rosewater
> 4 sweet apples
> 1 tbs lemon juice
> sugar to equal weight of the apples
> pinch of saffron

Remove the seeds from the cardamom pods, but do not crush, leave whole.

Peel and core the apples. Halve, then quarter them, then cut into two again making eight slices and sprinkle with the lemon juice.

Place the apples with the lemon juice and the sugar in a pan and add about 6 tablespoons of water. Bring to a boil, removing any scum which may form. Boil gently until the apples are just soft and take on a sort of translucent look.

Now add a good pinch of saffron and the cardamom seeds to the apples and their syrup. Boil for a few more minutes until the syrup is starting to set, then remove from the heat and leave to cool. Place in clean, dry jars and store in a cool place or the refrigerator.

MAKES ABOUT 2 ONE-POUND JARS

MURABA-E-ZANJAFEEL
Ginger Jam

This is another jam or preserve which is often served with yogurt as a snack or dessert, although it can be eaten with bread.

12 oz fresh ginger
2 cups sugar
½ tsp ground green cardamom
2 tbs lemon juice
½ tbs slivered or chopped almond and pistachio (optional)

Peel the ginger and then either grate or shred it in a food processor. Place in a pan and add 1 cup water. Bring to a boil and boil gently until soft. Add the sugar and cardamom, boil on a high heat and just before it starts to set add the lemon juice and the almonds and pistachios, if used. Boil for a few more minutes until the jam is firm and set. Allow to cool, then store in clean, dry jars. Keep in a cool place or a refrigerator.

MAKES ABOUT 2 ONE-POUND JARS

MURABA-E-KADU
Pumpkin Jam

This jam is a beautiful orange color and the cardamom seeds lend a lovely flavor.

2 lbs pumpkin
2 lbs oranges
60 cardamom pods
3 cups + 6 tbs granulated sugar

Remove the skin of the pumpkin. Also remove the inner seeds. Cut the flesh into ¾-inch cubes. Peel the oranges, removing as much pith as possible and cut into matchstick-size strips. Extract the juice from the oranges. Remove the seeds from the cardamom pods and reserve.

Place the pumpkin, orange juice, orange strips, sugar and whole cardamom seeds in a large pan, mix well and leave to marinate for about 10 hours or overnight. Stir occasionally.

Bring the mixture to a boil, then reduce the heat and simmer until the liquid has thickened and become syrupy. This can take about an hour or a little bit longer.

Leave to cool then place in clean, dry jars.

MAKES 3 TO 4 ONE-POUND JARS

An Afghan tea-vendor with his samovar.

Beverages

TEA

No Afghan cookery book would be complete without mentioning tea, *chai,* which is an important feature of the way of life. It is consumed in great quantities and I must say both the green and black tea are excellent. Afghan tea is particularly refreshing on the hot, dry summer days.

Tea is seldom drunk with milk but is often flavored with cardamom. On formal occasions, such as weddings and engagements, a special green tea called *qymaq chai* is prepared and drunk. *Qymaq,* a sort of clotted cream, is added to the top of the tea. A similar tea called *sheer chai* is prepared in the same way but without the *qymaq.* Salt is sometimes added instead of sugar to this tea, and it is served with various biscuits or bread such as *roht* or *nan-e-roghani.*

The hospitality of the people can be almost overwhelming at times. A good example of this is the honor attributed to a guest being measured by the amount of sugar he is given with his tea— the more sugar, the more honor. Another Afghan custom is to have a first cup of tea with sugar, *chai shireen,* followed by another cup without sugar. This second cup is called *chai talkh.* Many people soak sugar cubes called *qand* in their tea which they then hold in their mouths as they sip the tea.

Tea is often served with sweets, called *shirnee,* including *noql. Ghur,* a kind of lump sugar made from sugar cane, is also taken with tea, especially in the winter.

Another custom often observed is the turning over of your cup when you do not want any more tea. If you fail to do this, the host or hostess will continue to refill your cup with fresh, hot tea.

Because tea plays such an important role there are many *chaikhana,* tea houses, in Afghanistan. Apart from serving tea from a constantly boiling *samovar* they also provide other basic food and requirements for the traveler, for instance a simple and basic soup called *sherwa-e-chainaki.* This soup is actually made in a teapot, hence the name, teapot soup. The tea served in a *chaikhana* can be either black or green and is sometimes served in glass tumblers, but more often in handle-less porcelain bowls, similar to the Chinese tea bowl. Each customer has his own small teapot plus a small bowl for the dregs. When the tea is served, the customer rinses out his glass or bowl with the hot tea and pours this into his dregs bowl. Then he puts sugar, usually quite a lot, into his glass and adds fresh, hot tea. There are no chairs in a *chaikhana* so people sit around, cross-legged, on rugs and carpets on a specially constructed, raised, platform. The walls are also covered with carpets and pictures and there is usually popular Afghan or Indian music playing in the background which can be quite loud.

Teapot Soup.

MILK

Milk is scarce in the cities, and expensive; powdered milk is a common substitute. Milk is obtained from cows, water buffaloes, goats and sheep. In the countryside most families maintain at least one goat for producing milk, but without refrigeration this is difficult to keep; so milk products such as yogurt (*mast*), strained yogurt (*chaka*), dried yogurt (*quroot*), butter (*maska*) and cheese (*panir*) are made. *Qymaq* is a luxury milk product akin to clotted cream. A refreshing and popular drink in the summer is *doogh*, a combination of yogurt, mint, cucumber and salt.

Koumiss is an intoxicating beverage made from fermented mare's milk. It is still drunk in many parts of Central Asia but in Afghanistan because of its alcohol content it is now forbidden. Mountstuart Elphinstone in his *Account of The Kingdom of Caubul* describes how the national beverage of the Uzbeks was *kimmiz*:

> an intoxicatiang liquor, well known to be prepared from mare's milk. The milk is put in the afternoon into a skin, such as is used in India for holding water, and is allowed to remain till within two or three hours of day-break, when it is beaten and rolled about till morning at least; but the longer the better. The liquor thus made is of a whitish colour and a sourish taste: it is only to be had in plenty during the two last months of summer, and those who can afford it are generally drunk for the greater part of that period; but kimmiz is not sold, and those only can enjoy it who has mares enough to make it in the house.

SHRUBS AND OTHER BEVERAGES

Fruit juices, shrubs and syrups are made from a number of fresh fruits all year around. In the summer refreshing drinks are made from fruits in season such as peaches, cherries and pomegranates. Autumn brings further delights such as the quince. Oranges, both sweet (called *malta*) and Seville (called *norinj*) make popular drinks during the winter months. The juice of the sour Seville orange, and also lemon, is often sprinkled on *chalau* and *pilau* and on salads, for added flavor. *Kishmish ab*, a simple drink made from raisins is often purchased from street vendors. Rosewater, considered cooling and good for stomach complaints is often used to flavor drinks of lemon and other fruits. *Sekanjabin* is a very traditional drink made with mint.

In the grape producing areas, for instance north of Kabul, the juice from grapes leftover at the end of the season is extracted and kept in a cool place ready for drinking.

Afghanistan is a Muslim country and therefore alcoholic beverages, including wine, are not consumed. However, due to the rich variety and quality of the grapes, a wine factory was set up in the Puli Charkhi area of Kabul in the early 1970s and, with Italian assistance, wines for export were produced.

QYMAQ CHAI
Tea with Heavy Cream

This is a special tea prepared for formal occasions, such as engagements or weddings. It is made with green tea and by the process of aeration and the addition of baking soda the tea turns dark red. Milk is added (and sugar too) and it becomes a purply-pink color. It has a strong, rich taste.

Qymaq, the luxury cream-like product, is floated on the top. My husband, who is very poetic and very homesick, likens the color of the tea to the rosy-hued glow of the mountains in Afghanistan as the sun rises or sets. The *qymaq* represents the white snowcapped peaks. Commercial heavy cream can be used as a substitute although I have found the taste and texture are not quite the same and the heavy cream tends to dissolve quickly in the hot tea.

FOR THE *QYMAQ*:
2 cups whole milk
6 tbs heavy cream
½ tbs cornstarch

Add the milk to a pan and bring to a boil. Reduce heat and stir in the cream. Sift in the cornstarch, stir to mix, then whisk until frothy. Leave on a low heat for a couple of hours. A thick skin will form on the top of the milk. This should be removed from time to time and collected in another pan until there is only a small amount of milk left. This can take several hours. Place the pan with all the collected *qymaq* again on a very low heat and leave for a couple of hours more. Then keep the *qymaq* in a cool place until it is needed.

FOR THE TEA:
6 tsp green tea
¼ tsp baking soda
ice cubes
1¼ cups milk
4 - 8 tsp sugar, according to taste
1 - 2 tsp ground cardamom
8 tsp *qymaq*

First of all make the *qymaq* as described above and set aside in a cool place.

Put 3 cups water in a pan and bring to a boil. Add the green tea and boil for about 5 minutes until the leaves have opened up. Add the baking soda and continue to boil for a couple of minutes more. The tea will rise to the top of the pan while boiling. Each time it does add an ice cube to reduce the temperature. Remove the pan from the heat and allow the tea leaves to settle. Strain off and discard the tea leaves.

Put an ice cube into another pan and pour the tea into it from a height in order to aerate the tea. (A ladle could also be used to do the aeration, see the illustration below). Repeat, pouring from a height from pan to pan, several times, adding an ice cube each time until the tea becomes a dark red color.

Put the pan back on the heat and add the milk. The tea will now be a purply-pink color. Slowly heat it to just below boiling point, then stir in the sugar and cardamom according to taste.

Pour the tea into teacups and float 2 teaspoons of *qymaq* on top.

MAKES 4 CUPS

QYMAQ CHAI

CHAI-E-ZANJAFEEL
Ginger Tea

Ginger is considered a "hot" food and thought to be very good for curing stomach complaints and rheumatism. It is believed to increase the circulation of blood.

   3 tsp green tea
   2 tbs brown sugar
   2 - 3 tsp ground ginger
   1 tbs walnuts, very finely chopped or ground

Bring 3½ cups water to a boil in a pan, then add the tea and sugar. Continue boiling for about 2 minutes, then strain. Pour the tea back into the pan and add the ground ginger and walnuts. Bring back to a boil and boil again for about 2 minutes. Serve in teacups.

MAKES 4 CUPS

SHARBAT-E-OLU BOLU
Sour Cherry Shrub Drink and Conserve

In typical Afghan style nothing is wasted in this recipe. It is really two recipes in one, as a cherry conserve is made out of the residue from the drink. If sour cherries are not available, substitute sweet black cherries but add 2 tablespoons of lemon juice when bringing to a boil.

FOR THE SHRUB:
1 lb (500 g) sour cherries
2½ cups sugar

FOR THE CONSERVE:
the residue from boiling the cherries
½ cup of the shrub
½ cup sugar
lemon juice
½ tsp ground cardamom

Remove the stems and wash and stone the cherries. Place in a pan with the sugar and 2½ cups water. Bring slowly to a boil, allowing the sugar to dissolve. When boiling, reduce the heat and simmer for 40 to 45 minutes or until the juices have thickened and are a little syrupy. Strain, reserving the residue. Allow to cool before pouring into clean jars or bottles. Store in the refrigerator.

To serve, pour about couple of tablespoons of the concentrated juice over ice cubes and dilute further with chilled water.

TO MAKE THE CONSERVE: Place the cherry residue in a pan, add the shrub and the sugar. Add a good squeeze of lemon juice and the cardamom. Bring to a boil and continue boiling gently for about 3 minutes or so until a syrupy consistency has formed. Cool and store in clean dry jars.

This is delicious served with yogurt or ice cream.

MAKES 1 TO 2 ONE-POUND JARS

SHARBAT-E-BOMYA
Rosewater and Lemon Shrub

The rosewater and lemon combine wonderfully to make a refreshing summer drink.

    2¼ cups sugar
    1 cup lemon juice
    ½ cup rosewater

Place the sugar, 1 cup water and the lemon juice in a pan and over a medium/high heat bring to a boil, stirring often until the sugar has dissolved. Boil gently for about 2 minutes. Remove from the heat and leave the syrup to cool a little before adding the rosewater.
    Strain and serve in glasses diluted with ice cubes or crushed ice.
    For a pleasing effect decorate with small rose petals.

SERVES 4 TO 6

SHARBAT-E-RAYHAN
Basil Seed Shrub

Sharbat-e-rayhan is traditionally served with *shola-e-zard* (see p. 227) on the tenth day of *Muharram*. Basil seeds can be found in Thai supermarkets and some Asian supermarkets sell them under the name *tukmuria*.

    ¼ - ½ tsp basil seeds
    10 tbs warm water
    3 tbs sugar
    2 cups cold water
    1 - 2 tbs rosewater

First wash the basil seeds and soak them in the warm water for about 10 to 15 minutes. (The seeds will 'open out.') Put the sugar in a bowl and add the cold water. Stir to dissolve the sugar, then add the rosewater, the basil seeds and the water they were soaked in. Mix well and serve over ice cubes in individual glasses. You may add more sugar according to taste.

SERVES 4 TO 6

 ## SHARBAT-E-NORINJ
Orange Shrub

Seville oranges, if in season, are usually used to make this very refreshing drink. However, sweet oranges (called *malta*) can be substituted, although the taste will not be quite the same and the amount of lemon juice should be doubled to 4 tablespoons.

    2 cups fresh orange juice
    peel of 2 oranges
    2 tbs fresh lemon juice
    2¼ cups sugar

Remove as much pith as possible from the orange peel and cut into matchstick-size pieces.

Place all the ingredients in a pan with 2 cups water. Slowly bring to a boil allowing the sugar to dissolve. Now continue to simmer gently for about half an hour or until the juice has thickened a little and become syrupy.

Remove from the heat and allow to cool. Strain and pour into clean bottles or jars and seal. Store in the refrigerator.

To serve pour over ice cubes and stir in cold water to taste.

SERVES 4 TO 6

KISHMISH AB
Raisin Drink

Street vendors sell this refreshing, sweet drink on hot summer days. They serve the raisins and their juice in a small bowl or glass, the raisins being scooped up with a spoon. It is extremely simple to make.

8 oz golden or dark raisins
water

Wash the raisins well and place in a glass pitcher or bowl. Add water to cover by about 1 inch. Leave in a cool place or in the refrigerator for 2 to 3 days until the juice is sweet, stirring from time to time.

Serve the raisins with plenty of juice in individual glasses.

SERVES 4 TO 6

SEKANJABIN
Mint Shrub

When I served my mother-in-law mint sauce with roast lamb she told me it reminded her very much of the shrub drink they used to prepare in Afghanistan and gave me the following recipe. She also told me that it was often used for medicinal purposes, to help cure jaundice. It is a refreshing drink for hot, dusty summer days and street vendors sell it to weary people on their way home from work.

Sekanjabin can also be served undiluted with cos or romaine lettuce as a snack.

2½ cups sugar
½ cup + 2 tbs white wine vinegar
5 large sprigs mint, plus extra for decoration

Bring 1¼ cups water to a boil with the sugar in a pan, stirring often until the sugar has dissolved. Add the vinegar and bring to a boil, then simmer for about 20 minutes. Remove from the heat and submerge the sprigs of mint in the syrup. Leave to cool.

To serve as a drink, fill a glass with about one quarter to one third with the syrup, then top with cold water and ice cubes. Decorate with a fresh sprig of mint.

To serve as a snack, pour in a small bowl accompanied by another dish containing crisp cos lettuce leaves. The lettuce leaves are dipped into the shrub, scooping up some of the juice and are then eaten.

SERVES 4 TO 6

DOOGH

Yogurt and Mint Drink

Afghans enjoy drinking a cooling glass of *doogh* on hot summer days. It is mildly soporific.

    16 oz yogurt
    5-inch cucumber, peeled and grated (or finely chopped)
    2 tbs finely chopped fresh mint
    1 tsp salt

Add 4 cups water to the yogurt in a large jug. Add the cucumber, fresh mint and salt. Stir well (some people whisk the ingredients). Keep in the refrigerator until ready to serve. Ice cubes may be added although the taste will be diluted.

SERVES 6 TO 8

DOGH

Index

The Hippocrene Cookbook Library

Afghan Food & Cookery
African Cooking, Best of Regional
Albanian Cooking, Best of
Aprovécho: A Mexican-American
Border Cookbook
Argentina Cooks!
Australia, Good Food From
Austrian Cuisine, Best of, Exp. Ed.
Belgian Cookbook, A
Brazilian Cookery, The Art of
Bulgarian Cooking, Traditional
Burma, Flavors of,
Cajun Women, Cooking With
Calabria, Cucina di
Caucasus Mountains, Cuisines of the
Chile, Tasting
Colombian, Secrets of Cooking
Croatian Cooking, Best of, Exp. Ed.
Czech Cooking, Best of, Exp. Ed.
Danube, All Along The, Exp. Ed.
Dutch Cooking, Art of, Exp. Ed.
Egyptian Cooking
Eritrea, Taste of
Filipino Food, Fine
Finnish Cooking, Best of
French Caribbean Cuisine
French-English Dictionary of
Gastronomic Terms
French Fashion, Cooking in the
(Bilingual)
Greek Cuisine, The Best of, Exp. Ed.
Gypsy Feast: Recipes and Culinary
Traditions of the Romany People
Haiti, Taste of
Havana Cookbook, Old (Bilingual)
Hungarian Cookbook
Hungarian Cooking, Art of, Rev. Ed.
Icelandic Food & Cookery
Indian Spice Kitchen
International Dictionary of Gastronomy
Irish-Style, Feasting Galore
Italian Cuisine, Treasury of (Bilingual)
Japanese Home Cooking
Korean Cuisine, Best of

Laotian Cooking, Simple
Latvia, Taste of
Lithuanian Cooking, Art of
Macau, Taste of
Mayan Cooking
Middle Eastern Kitchen, The
Mongolian Cooking, Imperial
New Hampshire: From Farm to Kitchen
Norway, Tastes and Tales of
Persian Cooking, Art of
Peru, Tastes of
Poland's Gourmet Cuisine
Polish Cooking, Best of, Exp. Ed.
Polish Country Kitchen Cookbook
Polish Cuisine, Treasury of (Bilingual)
Polish Heritage Cookery, Ill. Ed.
Polish Traditions, Old
Portuguese Encounters, Cuisines of
Pyrenees, Tastes of
Quebec, Taste of
Rhine, All Along The
Romania, Taste of, Exp. Ed.
Russian Cooking, Best of, Exp. Ed.
Scandinavian Cooking, Best of
Scotland, Traditional Food From
Scottish-Irish Pub and Hearth Cookbook
Sephardic Israeli Cuisine
Sicilian Feasts
Slovak Cooking, Best of
Smorgasbord Cooking, Best of
South African Cookery, Traditional
South American Cookery, Art of
South Indian Cooking, Healthy
Spanish Family Cookbook, Rev. Ed.
Sri Lanka, Exotic Tastes of
Swiss Cookbook, The
Syria, Taste of
Taiwanese Cuisine, Best of
Thai Cuisine, Best of, Regional
Turkish Cuisine, Taste of
Ukrainian Cuisine, Best of, Exp. Ed.
Uzbek Cooking, Art of
Wales, Traditional Food From
Warsaw Cookbook, Old

www.ingramcontent.com/pod-product-compliance
Lightning Source LLC
Jackson TN
JSHW011354130125
77033JS00023B/681